ON THE

M000296516

A HISTORY OF SUGAR IN FLORIDA

by Nicholas G. Penniman IV

* "On the knife" is a common phrase among cane harvesters in the sugar fields with machetes and heavy leg guards to keep from cutting themselves.

No part of this publication may be reproduced in whole or in part, or stored in a retrieval system, or transmitted in any form or by any means, electronic, mechanical, photocopying, recording, or otherwise, without written permission of the author, except for the inclusion of brief quotations in a review.
For information regarding permission, please write to: info@barringerpublishing.com

Copyright © 2021 NICHOLAS G. PENNIMAN IV
All rights reserved.

Barringer Publishing, Naples, Florida
www.barringerpublishing.com
Design and layout by Linda S. Duider

On the cover:
Jemander. *Machetero*. Acrylic on Canvas. 16x24 inches.
Purchased by author in Santiago, Cuba, March 2014.

ISBN 978-1-954396-01-2

Library of Congress Cataloging-in-Publication Data
On The Knife
A History of Sugar in Florida

Printed in U.S.A.

FOREWORD

My interest in sugar began after moving to southwest Florida in 2000. Being involved in environmental advocacy, both in restoration of the historic Everglades and in land management issues, the subject came up again and again. What I soon learned was that the industry that controlled hundreds of thousands of acres was enormously powerful in the Congress and state legislature.

I have tried to write this book in the best tradition of my journalistic career, to tell all sides of a story and to seek out the hidden elements that are not immediately apparent or available. The telling of history is always fraught with one problem; it is written by the winners. Parts of the history of sugar in Florida involve controversy where there are no winners, so I sought primary sources to challenge common assumptions and the prevailing wisdom. One person I knew, and had debated against in public forums, was Judy Sanchez, Senior Director of Communications and Public Affairs for the U.S. Sugar Corporation based in Clewiston. Having a number of questions, some of which related to the mechanics of growing and harvesting of sugar, and others relating to her company's take on controversial issues, I sought her advice in an email. Here is what came back:

> Nick – *As I suspected, none of your questions seem to have anything to do with "fair looks" or the "history" of sugar in Florida. Seems you're penning just another piece of tabloid drivel built around the usual activist soundbites. There's really no need to tax yourself by doing much research for that. Just interview your cronies at the Foundation and those they've hired in their various echo chambers. So, we're out. Good luck with your "book."* . . . Judy

This is just an example of the defensive bulwark that has been built around the big sugar agro-industry to rebuff any attempt to open up their operations to outside scrutiny. This is a right given to a privately held corporation, but not to one beholden to the government for its profits. There seems to be no way around it.

In order to be fair, I then attempted to contact the Sugar Association but received no response to my questions.

One of the hazards in writing about controversial subjects is the tendency to look for confirming evidence and then use it alone; it's called cherry-picking. I have tried to avoid that, but in the case of sugar it is difficult because much of the "evidence" produced that supported industry positions has been paid for by sugar and confectionery companies. So, I have attempted to rely upon unbiased studies from government agencies like the General Accounting Office, the FDA and respected institutions like the American Heart Association and the American Diabetes Association.

For additional information and context, I would suggest reading Gail Hollander's *Raising Cane: The Global Sugar Trade and the Transformation of Florida* and Alec Wilkinson's *Big Sugar: Seasons in the Cane Fields of Florida.* The first is a superb example of good history and the second, a shattering exposé of the abuses heaped upon migrant cane cutters in south Florida.

Medical advice and review was provided by Dr. Steve Mason, a cardiologist and Dr. Steve Preston a nephrologist. On Everglades' issues, I relied upon the expertise of Dr. Steve Davis and Dr. Melodie Naja at the Everglades Foundation. Much of the early history of sugar comes from secondary sources. I visited Clewiston, Belle Glade and Okeechobee to get a feel for the cane fields and the nearby communities dedicated to sugar production.

I am grateful to Jeff Schlesinger of Barringer Publishing for his guidance and assistance in putting all the pieces of this book together with an accompanying web site, distribution and promotional materials. He has been a joy to work with as has graphic designer Linda Duider.

Finally, my wife Linda will have her husband of fifty-four years back again, willing to devote time and energy to our shared commitment to making southwest Florida into a better place for all.

TABLE OF CONTENTS

INTRODUCTION

The history of cane sugar in America is tangled and tawdry.

The tale begins in the pre-Revolutionary era when British interests controlled a large part of the Caribbean and actively fostered the slave trade. It moves through the Civil War and ensuing years with indentured labor until machines begin to take over much of the work done by stooped workers, chopping away at the lowest level of the plants while fighting heat, humidity, mosquitoes and snakes.

The human element aside, cane sugar has always enjoyed preferred status among the array of crop agriculture as to taxation, protection and various forms of financial subsidies since the 1700s. It has been inexorably involved in politics, the wellspring of those protectionist measures and it continues to this day. Despite the cries of free market advocates who find the sugar industry anomalous to the American sense of capitalism as a competitive enterprise, subsidies in the form of forgiven loans to processors continues to the present day.

And finally, as the United States population grows fatter by the year, health advocates and epidemiologists look to sugar in its various forms extracted from corn, beets and cane as one of the drivers of the obesity epidemic that plagues our society and eventually leads to an enormous toll of life and unnecessary depletion of health care resources.

The story of sugar in America has been told many times and in many ways. But the telling never ends because the industry is always justifying its profitable existence which is guaranteed by the federal government, not by reason but by obfuscation—through back door deals, money spread liberally around the halls of Congress and diffusion of the facts surrounding the health crisis in this country.

That's what this book is all about.

Early History of Sugar Across the Known World

Cane sugar is very old. Taxonomically, the earliest subspecies of the sugarcane plant genus was *Saccharum robustum.* Once domesticated it became *S. officinarum.* Over time it continued to be hybridized to maximize sucrose content by adapting to the soil and climate of cane growing areas throughout the world.[1]

Historians vary somewhat in their temporal estimates but are generally agreed that it originated in Southeast Asia, cultivated by natives of Papua, New Guinea, as early as 8000 BCE (Before Current Era). It may have spread throughout the southern Pacific as early as 6000 BCE, then to India about the same time. Its appearance in Indonesia is controversial; it may have been either imported from another source or more likely cultivated from wild indigenous plants.

In the oral tradition of those early Asian societies, cane sugar took on multiple personalities, one as the origin of the human race resulting from sexual consort between the first man and a stalk of cane—producing the human species. A similar myth exists within the cultures of certain Pacific peoples: one, that the primogenitor parents of the race were two sprouts of the same cane sugar shoot which after mating produced the human race. Another, that humans began their existence as separate cane shoots from different plants, both male and female.[2]

The significance of India is that mention of sugar appears in one of the first written languages of mankind— as a food and drink additive. The Sanskrit word for "sugar" is *sharkara* which can also be translated as "gravel" or "sand" an appropriate description of the granulated product. Later, with the establishment of trading routes between the east and west, India was the first country to produce sugar in granulated form, by drying cane juice sometime around 350 AD.

With a granulated product that could be stored and easily carried, Indian sailors, Arab traders, and traveling Buddhist monks began to spread sugar across their known world into the Mediterranean. With the product, traders brought information about the technique of refining cane.

But opportunities to grow, harvest and refine cane sugar were limited by geography because the cultivation, processing and growing of sugar requires two climatic elements: hot weather and lots of rain (or readily available water). For example, in Florida, it takes between 520 and 680 pounds of water to produce one pound of sugar, which calculates to between 62 and 81 gallons.[3] The Arab world, with warm temperatures and irrigation, was an ideal place to grow and process sugar during the fourteenth and fifteenth centuries, with merchants and traders selling it throughout Europe as a luxury item at prices similar to spices from the Orient.

SUGAR IN THE NEW WORLD

In his second voyage in 1493, Christopher Columbus carried seeds of the sugar plant to the new world where, in the Caribbean, it would grow and thrive.

The spread of sugar throughout the Caribbean was swift. Introduced into Brazil by Portuguese traders around 1500 AD, that country quickly became the most dynamic cane producer in the western hemisphere. By the mid-sixteenth century, there were over 2,000 operating mills in Brazil and another 1,000 in the Caribbean including the British Indies and Virgin Islands.

The British eventually controlled the most rapidly developing parts of the North American continent and found that sugar was one of the most lucrative resources to come from the Caribbean. But, the work of growing, cutting and processing sugar cane was labor-intensive and European diseases brought by the Spanish and British were decimating indigenous people who had been enslaved and ruthlessly used for sugar production. The declining population of locally available workers eventually led to the African slave trade and the notorious Triangle.

The Triangle was the name given to a three continent maritime passage from Britain carrying trade goods to Africa, slaves being transported from that continent to the Caribbean and sugar being immediately loaded and shipped to Britain for sale and distribution in Europe. This tripartite arrangement resulted in somewhere between eleven and thirteen million slaves being removed from their homeland in Africa and placed in squalid ships. They ended up in insufferable working conditions where a human life had less value than one stalk of cane.

FLORIDA: AS A BRITISH AND SPANISH COLONY

Florida, since Ponce de Leon's visit in 1513, remained more or less under Spanish control until the Treaty of Paris in 1763, ending the Seven Years War. As part of the settlement, Spain agreed to cede control of Florida to the British. Florida had been important to Spain as a source of cattle, but more as a critical, military buffer to the growing British presence in North America. The British, on the other hand, wanted to control the ports along Florida's coast, forcing Spanish vessels into the open water shipping lanes where they would fall prey to the British naval superiority and sponsored privateers.

Control of Florida switched back to Spain two decades later with the agreement that Great Britain would take over the Bahamas and Gibraltar in exchange for Florida. This followed the Spanish capture of Pensacola in 1781 and established a military presence in the panhandle that spread all the way to New Orleans and cut off the British from attacking American forces engaged in the Revolution.

The first known appearance of cane sugar plants in what would later become the United States of America was in 1751 when Jesuits brought plants from the Caribbean to New Orleans. This area was blessed with rich alluvial soil, warm weather year-round and abundant rainfall. Fourteen years later, the Spanish Governor of Florida, Pedro Menendez, attempted to grow cane in St. Augustine (which would later become the oldest city in the nation). Menendez was one of the originators of the *encomienda*, a system where the Spanish crown granted colonists the right to demand compensation, and labor, from indigenous people. But despite the free labor, commercial attempts to grow the crop failed with marginal weather, unsuitable soil and adverse climate conditions in the northeastern corner of the then colonial territory.

The first sugar refinery, using imported raw sugar, was opened in 1689 on Liberty Street in New York City. Sugar could not be grown in the original thirteen colonies, so raw sugar had to be imported from British colonies in the Caribbean, but after the American Revolution, Louisiana became a reliable producer of raw sugar as refiners sprung up throughout the colonies. Cuba became a reliable source of raw sugar as well and by 1795 nearly 600,000 pounds of sugar was being refined in Massachusetts, Rhode Island, Pennsylvania, New York, and Maryland, in or near port cities.[4]

However, the new federal government needed money. To help fill the treasury, import duties were assessed on raw sugar in 1789; from that year forward, until the Civil War, tariffs on the full array of imported goods accounted for two-thirds of the federal government's gross receipts. A tariff on imported sugar coming into the U.S., with the exception of four years from 1890 to 1894, was a form of protectionism. The infant government of the United States needed to nurture small businesses with little reliance on imported goods. It also needed trading partners in an uneasy world where the British still dominated the seas and trading routes.

NEW SMYRNA EXPERIMENT

With the colonies having some refining capacity before the Revolution, interest in sugarcane farming grew. In 1768, the colony of New Smyrna was founded by a Scottish physician named Andrew Turnbull, taking financial advantage of the British crown's desire to grow a variety of semi-tropical crops in sovereign territory. Located in present-day Volusia County, Florida, the settlement of 1,300 souls attempted to grow indigo, hemp and sugarcane. If successful with the last, they could also distill rum. The settlers, basically indentured servants, came from the Spanish Balearic Island and Greece with little experience in growing crops in a semi-tropical environment. The colony managed to last for a decade but the population gradually collapsed, after being continually harassed by native raiding parties and insensitive overseers. Survivors, about 600 in number, moved north to St. Augustine. New Smyrna remained nearly abandoned for the next hundred years.[5]

New Smyrna might have survived had it been around for the Tariff Act of 1789. The newly-formed government in Philadelphia was hungry for revenue and the major European powers were all thrusting raw materials upon the United States. This prevented it from developing its abundant natural resources, while the country was trying to push forward with economic development. Among the items subject to tariffs was molasses, a sugar product imported mainly from the Caribbean and given a lower preferential rate to satisfy rum producers in the northeastern states. Moving molasses by ship up the east coast was a lot less costly than bringing in the product from Spanish-controlled plantations along the Mississippi River in present day Louisiana and up the Ohio to the limited few railheads at the time.

But the New Smyrna experiment was not over. In 1830, a New York financier named Henry Cruger bought 600 acres near the town and built sugar and sawmills on the land. The area was part of the Seminole territory and in 1835, a raiding party plundered the site, with the help of the plantation's slaves anxious to escape, burning the mill and cane fields. The property changed hands numerous times after that, but sugar was never part of the picture.

FITS AND STARTS IN FLORIDA

With back and forth political control between Great Britain and Spain, there was little opportunity to establish large and stable agricultural operations in Florida, particularly those requiring a large number of workers that might compete with crops from Cuba and the West Indies. The slave states to the north, present day Georgia and South Carolina, had been held tightly under British military control which rigorously enforced slaveholding. Florida, already populated with the native Seminoles, became the primary destination for blacks escaping to seek freedom. After the British forces finally left Savannah in 1782, Georgia became the fourth state to join the newly founded United States of America, by ratifying the Constitution.

The Spanish influence in Florida waned with the Louisiana Purchase of 1803. But in a perverse turn of events the British, having lost the War of 1812, aligned with the Spanish to create a military frontier along the northern border of Florida. By 1815, Americans, having had enough of the British, decided to take Florida by force to capture thousands of runaway slaves. Andrew Jackson invaded the Panhandle in 1817, seizing Pensacola and other Spanish towns which began the First Seminole War and led to the Transcontinental Treaty of 1821 which ceded Florida to the United States.

SEMINOLE WARS

After the treaty and during the period before the Civil War, a number of attempts were made to grow sugarcane in north and central Florida. Small sugar plantations sprung up in the northern half of the state along rivers emptying into the Atlantic, but with marginal success due to unstable climate conditions.

The presence of Seminoles and escaped slaves in the southern part of the state discouraged efforts there, but the central part of the state was subject to periodic winter freezes which destroyed cane plants sensitive to cold weather. The price of importing sugar from Caribbean countries made it attractive, but eyes were always looking south toward the large lake in the middle of south Florida with rich soil in the drainage basin and ideal climatic growing conditions.

The purpose of the Second Seminole War of 1835–1842 was to drive the Seminoles out of their government-drawn reservation land north of Lake Okeechobee. The government was hounded and egged on by speculators who saw financial opportunity in an agricultural paradise freed of Native American presence. The war was fought in south Florida, much in the Everglades, where over 2,000 soldiers lost their lives, either to the Seminoles or by their own hand from the daily onslaught of mosquitoes and water moccasins bringing about the Armed Occupation Act of 1842. This act was designed to encourage small farmers to settle in the northern part of Florida as a barrier against the still contested ground to the south.

Florida was granted statehood as a slave state in 1845, leading up to the Third Seminole War of 1849–1859, a prolonged battle of attrition against a small group of natives under the leadership of Osceola, who had taken refuge in the forbidding Everglades. The Seminoles neither surrendered nor signed a peace accord.

In many ways, the Third Seminole War was the result of an 1847 study done by Buckingham Smith, a wealthy St. Augustine lawyer. Smith, using documents dating back to the early Spanish explorers, concluded that the muck under the surface of the Everglades south of Lake Okeechobee could be used for the "...cultivation of sugar, rice, tobacco, cotton or corn...."[6] His prose, in a report to Treasury Secretary H. Walker, was flowery and lyrical, unlike the dry legalese of most government memos at the time. A number of military officers fighting in the war also noted the fertility of the land around the lake as suitable for dual purposes: growing sugarcane and to create a buffer against foreign powers holding sway in the West Indies and Cuba. However, it was Smith who was the first person to promote the Everglades openly and publicly for agriculture.

CIVIL WAR

Florida sugarcane was unaffected by the war, mainly because the industry was in its nascent stages in the northern part of the state in small plantations, with crude processing equipment and small economies of scale when compared to Louisiana and the Caribbean. More important, before the Civil War, cotton was king in Florida. It was the most desirable export for the British market and easier to grow and harvest, at a lower cost, than sugarcane.

Central Florida was still appealing as a possible location for sugarcane farming. One of the largest early experiments was the Yulee sugar mill in Homosassa. David Yulee, serving in both the House and the Senate, after Florida was granted statehood, owned over five thousand acres deeded to his family by the Spanish. Farming including citrus, cotton and sugar cane, all cultivated and harvested by one thousand slaves. The sugar mill operated from 1851 to 1864, supplying the Confederacy with sugar and rum during the Civil War, until Union forces burned the mill toward the end of hostilities.

The main impact of the war on the domestic sugar industry was in Louisiana. The Jesuits had brought sugarcane plants to New Orleans in the 1750s. A technique for granulating the syrup was invented by Etienne de Bore and with the processing plants easily co-located with the fields, cane plantations along the Mississippi River became commonplace to exploit the rich muck of river silt deposited over the centuries, and by 1845, Louisiana was producing almost 25% the world's cane sugar.

It was an unforgiving world, heavily populated by enslaved workers and their French planter overseers escaping the Haitian Revolution that ended in 1804. The need for new slaves was incessant, because the field and processing work were done under brutal conditions with no regard for human life. Cutting cane in the fields was done by men, oppressed by heat and humidity, with the constant danger of reaching down to feel the needle fangs of poisonous snakes and the trenchant whips of overseers on horseback. Work in the mills, with the clamor of grinding rollers and the heat of kettles, was carried on by women and children.

The Congress banned importation of slaves in 1807 so most workers came from people already in the United States. Others came from the pirate, Jean Lafitte, and his partner, Jim Bowie, smuggling Caribbean slaves into the sloughs and bayous of the Mississippi delta. In the fifty years leading up to the Civil War, over 125,000 slaves had been used and discarded by the Louisiana sugar barons. The death rate was so high and the birth rate so low, that New Orleans became the slave market of the south, with the buying and selling of human beings either ignored or blindly tolerated by the resident Jesuits who had introduced sugar to the American south in the first place.

Despite the use of slave labor to plant and harvest the crop, the taste for sugar was growing rapidly, even in New England, and by 1836, thirty-eight refineries were in operation in a number of American port cities on the east coast. This allowed for easy import and handling of raw sugar from the Caribbean and to a lesser extent Louisiana where sugar plantations were highly vulnerable at the moment of the bombardment of Fort Sumter in 1861.

Nearly half the state's population was enslaved, and the Union strategy depended heavily upon a blockade of all Confederate ports with New Orleans at the top of the list, shutting down the Mississippi River plantations and the delta to markets in Europe where the demand for sugar was at an all-time high. The Confederacy, pressed for resources during the entire war, was unable to export the harvest.

In addition to supply dropping like a rock, the industry quickly fell apart as slaves, when Union forces were nearby, escaped from the servitude of their plantation masters, and were eventually freed with the capture of New Orleans by Union Forces in 1862. Louisiana's cane brought to market fell from 177,000 tons in 1861 to 5,400 tons in 1864.[7]

The lack of Louisiana sugar on the market had two effects. First, it placed Cuba and the Caribbean in the catbird's seat, and second, it forced the price of sugar into an upward trajectory. Cuba, with over fifteen hundred plantations manned by slave labor, became the world's leading sugar producer generating nearly 800,000 tons during the war years which accounted for about one-third of the world's supply. American investors, sensing the financial potential of supplying sugar to the Union and Britain during the war, had looked longingly at the island but were blocked by the Spanish throne.

SUGAR DURING RECONSTRUCTION

During the period after the Civil War and up to the turn of the century, sugar was forced to look for ways to mechanize its farming practices. Sugar took a back seat in Florida to cattle ranches but America's sweet tooth kept growing. Sugar beet farming grew rapidly in the northern states and refineries in the east coast port cities were increasing their output but rising costs, of both labor and raw sugar began to squeeze smaller operations and low profits began to have an effect. The number of refineries declined from fifty-nine in 1870 to forty-two in 1875.

The main reason for low profits was the rising cost of raw sugar. With ratification of amendments to the U.S. Constitution in 1868, Florida and other states including Louisiana agreed to grant citizenship to the former, and now freed, slaves. With that, one of the major industries of the south, cotton, lost free labor and had to pay workers to either go into the fields to pick or work out sharecropping arrangements with freed blacks. The work continued to be hard and the pay low. But cotton could be picked by women and children, whereas cutting cane was only suitable for men, making it a more costly operation.

There was little competition for field hand jobs; foreign émigrés saw more productive opportunities further north in building canals and railroads as the country embraced manifest destiny and westward expansion. The idea of growing sugar in Florida remained remote, as timbering along with cattle became the dominant industries, during the latter period of Reconstruction. By 1877, with an agreement to pull all U.S. troops out of Florida, over 90% of African-Americans in the state were engaged in agriculture.

The period of Reconstruction was over and rebuilding the economies of southern states became a leading priority of the federal government and elected officials in Florida.[8]

Having always been considered the southern frontier of the United States, Florida's governors, beginning in the 1880s, embarked on a development strategy that included railroads along both coasts and drainage of much of the state's wetlands, swamps and marshes. In recognition of the vast agricultural potential of the state, and abetted by a sense of boosterism, Florida would make deals with anyone willing to set mind and money to either run tracks down along sandy beaches or to transform raw wet land into tillable fields of promise.

Before recounting how that happened, we need to turn to the fundamentals of botany, hybridization, harvest and production of sugar, from both cane and beets, to better understand how and why Florida's climate and soils gave it the perfect circumstances to become the largest sugar producing state in the nation.

Beet and Cane Fundamentals

BEET SUGAR

The beet as a source of sugar was discovered in 1747 by German chemist Andreas Margraaf, but it never made inroads into European agriculture, until the Napoleonic Wars when Great Britain blockaded the continent from receiving West Indies sugar. In response, a number of countries began to cultivate beets, but sporadic attempts to grow the root in the United States in the 1830s failed, mainly because Louisiana could produce raw cane sugar more cheaply using slave labor. Even with the main domestic sources shut down by the Civil War, it took until 1870 for the first beet processing plant to begin operations in Alvarado, California.

During Reconstruction, a number of Europeans immigrated to the United States. Finding the northern climates (Wisconsin and Nebraska) and the west coast most suitable they brought with them the seeds and knowledge to begin to grow the crop widely and profitably and by the turn of the century, there were twenty-nine plants in operation.

The growth of beet production, occurring over thirty years leading up to the turn of the century, was spread throughout twelve northern tier states from California to Michigan and gathered political power, mainly in the Senate, in the process. In the cane-producing region of the south, Louisiana was still dominant but recognized the importance of cooperating with beet sugar growers as their political leverage grew. With this alliance, much of the legislation introduced later, during the Great Depression, set the stage for contemporary sugar policy, but it originated primarily from representatives and senators in the beet growing states.

Beets are an annual crop and are members of the amaranth family. Planted in the spring in temperate climates, they are harvested in the late fall and early winter. They can be a rotational crop, used to preserve soil minerals, and require large land areas for cultivation. When sugar beets are used as a rotated crop, the normal cycle is every two years, with corn as a preferred follow-on. The growing period runs around six months with about twenty-four inches of rainfall or irrigation. Grown from seeds, beets can tolerate a wide variety of soils from loam to clay, when planted spaced three inches apart in furrows with about two feet between them. Finally, beet seeds can be planted in the spring and harvested in the fall, so the farmers could quickly adjust to demand for their product, or to any changes in government allotments on an annual basis.

The sugar beet has a large white root and is inedible, not like the delicious purple ones we use in our salads and as vegetables. Dug up by machine during the fall harvest season, the root is separated from the leaves and thoroughly washed. Taken to a processing plant, which does not have to be near the fields because the harvested root has a longer shelf life than sugarcane, particularly in a colder climate, the roots are sliced into thin pieces to increase the surface area from which to extract the sugar.

The sliced roots are then moved to a diffuser, an agitating tank that uses counterflow to move the pieces through the water, extracting both sucrose and other chemicals. Once removed from the diffuser, the slices are run through a series of rollers to squeeze additional saccharin from the beet pulp. The diluted juice is then chalked, in a process known as carbonatation. Once added, the chalk collects non-sugar chemicals and is subsequently filtered out. The remaining diluted juice is transferred to an evaporator to reduce the water content of the syrupy mix.

Finally, the syrup slurry is moved to a large pot where the remaining liquid is boiled off leaving a dry crystalline substance that is mixed with sugar dust and spun in a centrifuge to create pure sugar crystals.

CANE SUGAR—HOW PLANTED, GROWN, HARVESTED, AND REFINED

Sugarcane is a perennial grass grown in tropical and semi-tropical climates. It is planted by cuttings or cultivars, not seeds, spaced about eighteen inches apart. Each plant reaches an average of nine to twelve feet in height and is composed of three parts: root, stalk and leaves. Being photosynthetic, the plant is highly efficient at converting carbon dioxide (CO_2) into sugar using solar radiation and chlorophyll.

There are actually three different types of cane: chewing, crystal and syrup. Each has a different level of sugar, with crystal having the highest level of sucrose.

Sugarcane seeds are tiny. Until twentieth century research proved otherwise, it was widely believed that cane plants did not produce true seed. Growing on the tops of cane plants, the seeds do not have the genetic coding of the parent plant. With seed from some plants (most are sterile), cross-fertilization could create stronger, disease-resistant hybrids, with higher sucrose yields. But field planting from seed always remained impractical, so cuttings are always used. Those cultivars, short pieces of cane plants with buds, are then planted in furrows.

Once planted, each cultivar sprouts in a process called "tillering," and has an accelerated growth rate for about six or seven months, then slows for another few months to reach full maturity in anywhere between eight and twenty-four months, but then can last for up to four years through multiple harvests. Sugarcane requires eighty to ninety inches of water during the growing period and thrives with good drainage in a variety of soils.

Planted in rows about five feet apart, the stalks are cut at the stems either by machine or hand, above the root system to permit regeneration from the root. Sucrose, in the stalk, increases closer to the root and dries out quickly, so processing needs to take place in facilities located adjacent to the sugarcane fields. Cutting occurs between October and March, a period of about five months during the "dry season" in Florida and most of the Gulf Coast, because each field must be burned (depending upon weather conditions) and the machinery does not get bogged down in saturated soil.

Regrowth of each plant occurs through the root stubbles, called "ratoons" (from a Spanish verb *retoñar*), allowing multiple harvests from a single planting. A heavy leaf cover is desirable as it reduces weed growth between plants and furrows, and because weeding is done mainly by hand. Before harvest the fields are burned to reduce the canopy cover. Hand-cutting for the harvest is preferred because it is more precise but more expensive, while machine cutting is done with a series of rotating knives from the bottom of the stalk to the foliage at the cane top. The stalks are then cut into twelve-inch lengths and hauled to a processing facility.

The first step in processing is extraction—squeezing out the juice out using mangles, a series of rollers. The left over and compressed fibrous leaf and stem, called *bagasse*, was once used to make Celotex (a building material) but is now used to fuel boilers for steam-driven turbines and boiling. The CO_2 produced from burning is then partially consumed by the cane in adjacent fields encouraging photosynthesis.

The juice once squeezed out, containing dirt and small particles of extraneous matter from the field, is infiltrated with lime to settle out the undesirable byproducts, and then evaporated by reduction into a thick liquid by boiling off the water through a series of flasks to allow dirt to settle in the bottom as the syrup moves through the processing tanks.

The final stage is similar to sugar beet processing where the syrup is moved to a large boiling pot and salted with sugar dust to promote crystal formation. Once formed, the crystals are spun-dried into raw sugar and stored for the next step—refining.

Raw sugar isn't pretty. It's brown and sticky, so the job of refining is to make sure individual grains do not clump together and the final product, granulated sugar, appears clean and white. To do this, raw sugar goes through a series of steps in the boiling house where, in the jargon of the industry are: affination, carbonatation, filtration, and crystallization.

The first step is "affination," where raw sugar is mixed with heavy syrup of slightly higher purity (so it doesn't dissolve the crystals) and spun in a centrifuge to wash off the outer coating of molasses to expose the greater purity of the interior. The molasses is removed and can be used for other purposes, one of which is making rum.

The next step, "carbonatation," is done by re-dissolving the crystallized sugar into a syrup (about 60–70 percent solids) and achieved by a number of different techniques. One is to add a combination of phosphoric acid and calcium hydroxide to form precipitate calcium phosphate; another is to combine calcium hydroxide with carbon dioxide. The particles then engage a variety of solid and chemical impurities while absorbing others, and float them to the top of the tank, where they can be skimmed off. The liquid from dissolving the washed crystals contains solids, and gums with some sucrose but also nearly equal quantities of fructose and glucose.

The pH level is critical at this point, desirable at pH8. If it drops down to pH7, it hydrolyses the sucrose down to component glucose and fructose. At higher levels of alkalinity, the sugars are destroyed.

After any remaining solids are filtered out, the syrup is decolorized by filtration through the use of either bone char made from the bones of cattle, or activated carbon, a technique that changes the color but does little else. Another method uses ion exchange which does less for changing the color but removes some inorganics.

To produce granulated sugar, in which the individual grains do not clump together, sugar must be dried and the crystals separated from the mother liquid by centrifuging.

At this point in the process, the liquid medium is clear and ready for final crystallization.

To do this last step, the purified syrup, concentrated to supersaturation in mother liquor known as *massecuite*, is crystallized by boiling off all remaining liquid and then placed under vacuum pressure to produce white, refined sugar. It is dried in a hot, rotary unit, followed by forcing cool air through the crystals. The remaining liquor is discharged and reused. The crystals are then graded, packaged and ready for market.

MARKETING THE PRODUCT

Beet growers in the U.S. sign individual production contracts with processors each year, specifying the number of acres to be planted and harvested, while the seeds, types of fertilizer and date of expected harvest are supplied by the processor. There are three different types of contracts depending upon location, but the main point of dictating a date of harvest is to insure a steady flow of product into the mills.

The price to the grower is directly related to the price the processor receives, and to a measurement of the sucrose content extracted from the harvested beets. The Secretary of Agriculture has a set of criteria related to the sugar content in determining the price in the current system and sets a floor for processors to buy from their suppliers.

There were a relatively small number of beet processors, about six, bringing 90% of the final product to market in 1975, with some cross-ownership within that small group.[9] Currently four companies dominate the business: Western Sugar Cooperative, Michigan Sugar Company, Amalgamated Sugar and American Crystal Sugar Company. All are grower-owned cooperatives.

Cane sugar processing is also handled by a relatively small number of companies, consolidating over time by acquisition, merger and the tender mercies of the market. Much of the cane is farmed by large, vertically integrated conglomerates that have transportation, processing and refining under the same corporate umbrella, sometimes using wholly-owned subsidiary corporations.

For cane not farmed by the large corporations, contracts to purchase crops are mainly verbal, with the minimum price once again set by the Secretary of Agriculture. Over time, smaller famers joined together in co-ops, some building their own processing plants and others were selling to larger conglomerates with excess processing capacity. Since the system has become highly managed over the years, the early imbalances between demand and supply of harvested cane have been tightened so in the U.S. there is a symbiotic relationship between growers and processors.

Besides, the existence of small farmers helped the massive conglomerates make the argument that they were not monopolists, an argument to be made in spades as sugar legislation worked its way through Congress over the twentieth century.

Tariffs, Cuba and the Sugar Trust

After Reconstruction and during the Gilded Age, sugar policy in the U.S. was affected by a battle between free-trader advocates and protectionists advocating tariffs, a confused foreign policy with regard to Cuba and something called the Sugar Trust. The interaction of these forces, with political leadership in America shifting between the Democrat and Republican parties, created one of the major impediments for capital investment in sugarcane: uncertainty.

To set the stage, Cuba, controlled by the Spanish throne, dominated the world market for sugarcane. The United States economy was being overwhelmed by a small group of corporations exercising monopoly control over markets, and would undergo a massive, financial crisis in 1893 that determined the course of trade and tax policy for nearly a decade, as the country tried to pull out of a recession marked by near panic of a meltdown that would slide into recession.

TARIFFS IN THE GILDED AGE

The Gilded Age was markedly successful for a small number of businessmen as the railroads expanded westward, industrial development replaced agriculture as the mainstay of the American economy, politicians were bought and sold as chattel to prevent government interference in the emerging monopolies and money flowed upward to the privileged few.

Reactions to the excesses of the Gilded Age by those exploited by the robber barons was embodied in the Populist movement, the rise of labor unions, and passage of the Sherman Act in 1890, restricting corporate consolidation with the idea of breaking up monopolies.

At the height of the Gilded Age in 1890, a punitive tariff was passed sponsored by Republican Congressman William McKinley of Ohio. The tariff placed a heavy burden on manufactured goods coming from abroad but exempted certain products—refined sugar among them. However, to compensate for the possible loss of income from imports, beet sugar producers and sugarcane growers in Louisiana were granted a two cent per pound bounty. This was perceived as a gift to the business community and opposed by Democrats because it would open the American market to lower cost imported sugar. But it was also a disaster for Hawaiian growers.

The west coast sugar business was dominated at the time by the Spreckels Sugar Company. After the tariffs had been lifted on Hawaiian sugar in 1876, Spreckels began buying up small plantations throughout the islands and soon became the largest refiner on the west coast using raw sugar from Hawaii. The company was a voracious acquirer of refining operations too, buying out most of the competition in California and closing down their plants. But the McKinley tariff exemption mitigated the advantage of bringing in sugar from the islands, and Spreckels decided to come east to compete with the Havemeyer companies by building a huge refinery in Philadelphia. That decision was crucial, because it eventually created a monolith called the Sugar Trust.

The McKinley tariff cost Republicans the House and Senate that fall and the presidential election of 1892 when Grover Cleveland defeated the incumbent, Benjamin Harrison.

With sugar tariffs being a factor in the election, another more subtle campaign was waged by a staff member of the present-day United States Department of Agriculture (USDA). Being familiar with experiments at St. Cloud Plantation in Florida, the department's chief chemist, Harvey Wiley, offered his assessment of Florida's capacity to grow cane. In a theme to be repeated over and over, he waxed poetic:

"There is practically no body of land in the world which presents such remarkable possibilities of development as the muck lands bordering the southern shores of Lake

Okeechobee. With a depth of soil averaging perhaps 8 feet, and an extent of nearly half a million acres, with a surface absolutely level, it affords a promise of development which reaches the limits of prophesy." [10]

Harvey Wiley spent most of his life in an effort to engage government in oversight of America's food supply as related to public health. He was the creator of the Good Housekeeping Institute laboratory to ensure that the eponymous publication, created in 1885, published scientifically credible information as it became one of the top five magazines in the country. In 1927, he warned about the possible harmful effects of tobacco use. But in 1891, his interest was clearly in promoting the Everglades as the ideal location to grow American sugar and marked the first real involvement of a government agency in Florida's latent capacity, sparked by one of America's first pure food advocates.

One year later, the economy cratered. The Panic of 1893 was the worst recession in the history of the United States. Over 16,000 businesses and 640 banks failed. Railroads were particularly hard hit and employment plummeted.

TARIFF FRENZY

To stave off disaster, Congress passed the Wilson-Gorman Tariff Act of 1894. President Cleveland, a free-trade Democrat, supported the initial bill vowing to sign it as soon as it hit his desk, believing that a reduction in burdensome tariffs would bolster the American economy. But Gorman, a Maryland senator and one of the sponsors, began cutting deals behind the scenes. Groups from domestic wool growers to extraction industries like iron ore and coal carved their own protections into the bill. One of the particularly egregious amendments included further protection for domestic sugar by raising tariff rates on imports but was offset by eliminating the two cent per pound bounty for domestic production that had been installed in 1890. The bill was passed with Cleveland's signature but was nullified a year later, because it included a two per cent tax on incomes over a certain level, which was judged by the court to be unconstitutional.

Following the Crash of 1893 and with passage of the Wilson-Gorman Tariffs of 1894, it was argued in the national election that the easing of tariffs had prolonged the recession and a more protectionist posture was needed. Running on this platform, Republicans regained control of both the House and Senate in the 1896 election along with installation of William McKinley, author of the 1890 tariff plan, as president.

One of the first acts of the newly seated Congress was passage of the Dingley Act of 1897, a massive imposition of tariffs on almost every conceivable import. The tariffs represented an ad valorem increase of nearly 60% when all items were considered. In the case of sugar, the tariff on imported sugar doubled but for some reason the two cent per pound bounty was restored.

While the drama played out in the halls of Congress, foreign policy was being conducted with sugar as a major element, and the main victim of the tariff wars was a large island only ninety miles south of Key Largo.

CUBA

Cuba, by the middle of the nineteenth century, had become the largest producer of sugar in the Caribbean. Starting at about 55,000 tons in 1820, it was helped by Louisiana's production shut down during the Civil War. The island was possessed of an ideal climate, adequate water and cheap labor all of which went to foster growth of the industry, reaching a peak of over one million tons in 1895, just before the Spanish-American War of 1898. The Spanish-controlled island, just before the turn of the century, had become the world's largest cane sugar producer.

With the beginning of free trade in 1898, Cuba was the United States' largest supplier of sugar, continuing through the Smoot-Hawley Act of 1930 and despite the seemingly beneficial relationship between the two countries, the years were marked by a series of inconsistent policies because the American government used Cuba to balance irregularities in supply coming from domestic sources.

Beet sugar came onto the world market in 1747 with mechanical processing at the turn of the nineteenth century in Poland. One hundred years later, beet was providing over two-thirds of the world's sugar. But the beet sugar industry in the United States, while it was slow to develop before the turn of the twentieth century, played a pivotal role in the future of the cane sugar industry in America, and in the creation of a system of financial subsidy that would guarantee a profit for both sides of the business.

The story of how it happened is complicated.

SPANISH-AMERICAN WAR AND AFTERMATH

America's entry into the brief Spanish-American War of 1898 was in support of the Cuban revolution for independence from Spain. Led by Jose Marti, rebel forces, beginning in 1894, had continued to gather strength and support. While Cuba had been beset by small uprisings against Spanish rule in the past, the American presence was designed to help the revolution which had begun in the western provinces and was beginning to spread more widely throughout the country.

To add to the complexity of the situation, the revolution was as much against American imperialism as it was against the Spanish overlords. As the fighting in Cuba ground on, sugar plantations were being decimated and to add insult to injury the United States government, having recently voted in a Republican president and Congress, passed the Dingley Tariff of 1897 with full backing from beet sugar interests. The tariff added layers of protection to the domestic industry and drove a wooden stake into the heart of Cuban sugar production.

The United States had always been chary of the Spanish presence in Cuba. Relations were cordial but strained until the spring of 1898 when William Randolph Hearst started a war with what might be called today "fake news." Hearst, publisher of the *New York Examiner* was locked in a circulation battle with Joseph Pulitzer's *New York World*. And wars were big news.

Hearst was also a strong supporter of Theodore Roosevelt, whom he thought could be president, after getting a few military chops. At the time, the battleship Maine was anchored in Havana Harbor and was rocked by an internal explosion. Hearst seized upon the incident, declaring in a front-page headline that the damage had been from a Spanish torpedo designed to blow a hole in the hull of the Maine. In 1974, an inquiry discovered that the explosion was from a faulty boiler, but Hearst got his war with one of the first and worst incidents of what is known today as "fake news."

President McKinley then went before Congress with his war message in April 1898. It was passed by a joint resolution but then immediately modified by the Teller Amendment. Henry Teller was a Republican senator from Colorado, a beet sugar producing state. Beet sugar farmers in the northern tier of states, including Colorado, were vehemently opposed to Cuba, with its enormous potential and low costs for producing sugar, joining the union. With full-fledged statehood there would be no tariffs and no import quotas and the beet sugar industry would be exposed to free market forces. And the Teller Amendment would take care of that by ensuring that the United States, should it remove Spain from the island, could not annex Cuba or permit it to enter the union as a state.

While the war in Cuba was fought mainly on land, featuring Theodore Roosevelt charging up San Juan Hill with his notorious and well-publicized (thanks to Hearst) Rough Riders, the battle of Manila Bay, in May 1898, was more dramatic and meaningful in ending the hostilities. It eliminated the Spanish presence in the Philippines and Guam, and more importantly, checkmated the global expansionist plans of one of Europe's great powers. The war ended with the Treaty of Paris, negotiated in the winter of 1898 and ratified by the U.S. Congress the next spring. American troops occupied Cuba for four years but the subject of annexation, thanks to the beet sugar industry, never came up.

BEET FIGHTS CUBAN STATEHOOD

American investment in Cuba before the war had reached about $50 million and after the occupation by American military, rapidly increased. Business interests saw the financial gains ripe for the plucking in Cuba, and a series of military orders from General John Brooke enforced the rights of creditors to pursue collection of debts that sugar farmers could not satisfy. Most of the capital came from American lenders and small farmers were forced to sell their property to satisfy indebtedness. Cubans, on the other hand, ardently desired independence and were willing to, once again, fight for it.[11]

The possibility of a continuing revolution, since the Cuban people had little interest in annexation or American dominance of the island, chilled investment, and the idea died a quiet death when, in 1902, the Platt Amendment was passed guaranteeing American government enforcement of property rights in Cuba—using military force if necessary. The price for the amendment was withdrawal of U.S. forces and recognition of the new government formed by President Tomas Palma, but with the guarantee of military intervention, the United Fruit Company bought 180,000 acres in 1902 and another 204,000 acres in 1904.

It was a moment when politics backed by military force applied the Monroe Doctrine to the Caribbean and beyond. In the Pacific, Guam became an American protectorate, and its westernmost territory, with defeat of the Spanish at Manila Bay. Had annexation or statehood for Cuba been achieved, the sugar industry in the United States would have taken an entirely different trajectory. But the beet interests were strongly opposed, powerful and well-organized with support from a Republican Congress.

The techniques for growing and extracting sugar from beets came mainly from Europeans migrating to the U.S., mainly from Germany. The soils and climate were vastly different across the new country so development was slowed by trial and error but the political support was early and unified and suspicious of Cuba.

With firm opposition from beet-growing legislators, Cuba had no chance of being given preferred status and while the beet growing states held sway in Washington the largest effect was on the State of Florida. While protectionism was always a piece of the American character, the Republican administration in power at the time wanted sugar grown in the United States. The problem for the beet was that cane was cheaper and produced higher yields; in one hundred years, Harvey Wiley's prediction would appear prescient.

ENTER THE SUGAR TRUST

Toward the end of Reconstruction, a number of American businesses, preferring cooperation to competition, realized that there was a lack of government oversight and regulation and began to consolidate operations under a single economic entity. Power came from the ability to control prices in the market, and the sugar industry took advantage of the opportunity. It was called the Sugar Trust and was one of a number of business trusts in the United States toward the end of the Gilded Age.

In the case of sugar, the price differential between raw and refined sugar had dropped from 1.437¢ per pound in 1882 to 0.712¢ per pound in 1885. It held at that level for the next two years affecting the profitability of refiners. In response, the Sugar Trust was formed to prop up the price by controlling supply.

A new company, American Sugar Refining (ASR),

was formed in 1887 in Philadelphia. An innovator in sugar refining, its main plant had burned to the ground and the rebuilt facility in Brooklyn stood ten stories tall, with the adjoining filter house topping out at thirteen stories. The president, H. O. Havemeyer, better known as the "Sugar Pope," began consolidating support from competitors as quickly as possible. Each of eleven refiners immediately exchanged shares of their stock for trust certificates in ASR managed by eleven trustees. By 1889, the company controlled the shares of seventeen of the twenty-one refineries in the United States. As it absorbed new processing facilities, the trust was able to successfully manipulate output by closing certain plants and moving production around to operate at capacity (thus decreasing costs). As the amount of refined sugar on the market was carefully controlled by the Trust, the price increased. Profits were distributed among all participating companies; margins improved substantially. And with its low-cost operation, ASR was beginning to compete successfully on the West Coast against the powerful Spreckels Sugar Refining, by buying up smaller companies and even destroying equipment. It was raw competition with the intent of either destroying Spreckels or forcing a negotiation from a position of strength.

Spreckels' success depended heavily on raw sugar imported from the Hawaiian Islands. The company owned vast plantations there, dating back to 1876, but had been bounced around by the tariff wars of the 1890s. Hawaii cane growing was blessed by an 1875 agreement with the federal government that allowed its production to enter the United States duty-free, a deal attracting American investors like Spreckels. But when the 1890 act eliminated tariffs on imported sugar, Hawaiian sugar lost its advantage to Cuba and other Caribbean suppliers leading to a revolution against the monarchy on the islands and establishment of a republic leading to eventual annexation by the United States.

The Spreckels Company, led by ruthless entrepreneur Claus Spreckels also known as the "Sugar King of the Sandwich Islands," dominated the California and Northwest market and when the Trust entered his backyard by buying up his competitors, he decided to build a massive 176,000 sq. ft. refining plant in Pennsylvania in 1890 to compete with Havemeyer. He then split it off into another company which later, in a secret deal, allowed Havemeyer to buy a 45% interest in 1891 in exchange for which the Trust shut down its plant in California and Spreckels' investment was pooled with American Sugar Refining until all Spreckels shares were purchased by the Trust in 1895, allowing the newly combined operations control of over 90% of the refining capacity in the United States at the time and 97% by 1907. Spreckels doubled his money in the deal, but by competing with the Trust in Philadelphia, he was no longer regarded as a predatory monopolist on the West Coast, but rather as a victorious champion of free market competition.

In retrospect, it was the unpredictable nature of

import duties at the time, from the back and forth between free-trade Democrats and protectionist Republicans that brought the Spreckels family east to compete with the Havemeyer interests before combining forces to bolster the Sugar Trust. Cut from the same bolt of cloth, they were brutal businessmen fighting for a rapidly growing piece of a relatively small domestic market.

In 1866, right after the Civil War, sugar consumption in the U.S. was 440,000 tons; in 1896, it was 2.8 million tons. Around 14% was grown and processed on the mainland, up from 6% in 1866. Cuba was providing almost 50% until the Panic of 1893 when exports to the U.S. dropped sharply, but after that, American investment in Cuba began to pick up again encouraging trade to move back toward normal levels.

An important part of the Trust's agenda was to present a coherent political front. The Trust gave generously to the McKinley campaign in 1896. Sugar growers in Louisiana were also quietly supportive, and their combined rewards were highly protective tariffs in 1897 and a brief war against Spain in 1898, giving American sugar interests protection and easy entry into Cuba's vast and productive cane growing capacity as covered earlier in this chapter.

The government first filed suit against the Trust in Pennsylvania in 1892 alleging violation of the recently passed Sherman Act of 1890, arguing that the company was in reality a combination formed to restrain trade and control the price of sugar. The court ruled against the government with tortured logic, asserting that the act of incorporation occurred within the boundaries of the State of Pennsylvania and that federal law applied only to distribution where interstate commerce was involved and not to manufacturing operations like the refining of sugar.

Horrified by the decision, and the loss of a first appeal, government lawyers filed a case against the Trust on different charges, a case that ended up in the U.S. Supreme Court in 1894 where sugar won again.

As a further manifestation of the power and importance of sugar at the turn of the century, the American Sugar Refining Company was one of the original twelve stocks listed in the initial Dow Jones Industrial Average in 1896.

Another suit against the Trust was filed during the trust-busting era following the Gilded Age. In 1910, the government decided to break up the trust which by then was alleged to have thirty corporations involved in ownership, including the Cuban-American Sugar Company controlled by the National Sugar Company and jointly owned by the Havemeyer's and Spreckels' American Sugar Company. This was a sign that the sugar barons had decided that investing in Cuba, particularly after the Spanish-American War, was better than competing. The suit dragged on for eleven years and was settled in 1921 by consent decree, since the market share of the Trust had dropped below 25% as imports rose, and beet sugar began to take hold in the upper Midwest and world production came back strong after World War I.

One goal of the Sugar Trust was to keep refineries operating at their most efficient levels to maximize the price differential between raw and refined sugar. The Spreckels' interests in Hawaii and beet sugar growers in the U.S. were highly protective of their situation, particularly Spreckels who had vertically integrated operations to include growing, processing and refining. And the best way of doing this was to discourage foreign sources of raw sugar through tariffs.

Sugar at the turn of the century had gained enough political power to affect the course of history. Despite efforts by the government to break up the virtual monopoly created by the Sugar Trust, it was unsuccessful as the refiners were able to effectively overcome the government's legal challenges. Florida played little role at the time, mainly because the Platt Amendment of 1902, and the Reciprocity Treaty of 1903, minimized risk and encouraged U.S. money to move to Cuba and buy up raw land on the eastern end of the island. The 1903 agreement, supported strongly by President Roosevelt, formed the basis for trade for a generation. It gave Cuba, despite being denied statehood or territorial protection, a decided advantage even over tariff-free sugar coming in from Hawaii and the Philippines due in large part to the amount of American money invested in the island.

Florida Experiments Begin in Earnest

Cattle, cotton and timber were Florida's dominant industries during Reconstruction but a well-documented history of experimentation in growing sugar in Florida at the beginning of the Gilded Age involves the tale of Hamilton Disston and the St. Cloud Sugar Plantation.

Disston was a Philadelphia businessman and devoted fisherman. Florida's fresh-water bass lakes, with little pressure, had large fish eager to grab onto an angler's lure, bringing Disston to Florida beginning in the 1870s.

Also, in the 1870s, the Internal Improvement Fund (IIF) in Florida, with over 20 million acres of land ceded by the federal government to state control, was in bankruptcy receivership for claims owed. Governor William Bloxham, elected in 1881, was determined that the IIF regain financial stability and Disston, with his love of Florida, was approached by Bloxham to purchase 4 million acres for $1 million. The idea was to drain the central and southern part of the state, around Lake Okeechobee, to make it suitable for farming and development.

At the time, most of the cane sugar was grown in the northern part of the state, but the crop suffered from uncertain weather and high costs of labor, while Cuba was able to compete with slave labor until 1886 (when slavery was abolished by Spanish royal decree).

Looking south toward the central heart of the state, Disston decided to plant twenty acres of sugarcane in the Kissimmee watershed, south of present-day Orlando. With no fertilization and normal rainfall, the crop came in ready for harvest eleven months later at twelve feet high—impressive growth, extraordinary for the time. (Today, the normal height of hybrid sugarcane is about eight to twelve feet). Documents from the experiment indicate a high yield of 700 gallons of syrup per acre.

Disston was intrigued and redoubled his efforts to build canals to drain Lake Okeechobee and direct water to agricultural lands. In 1887, he bought a half-interest in the St. Cloud Plantation in Osceola County, and with his partner, Rufus Rose, expanded sugar growing and processing as quickly as they could with limited resources and few experienced field hands. Originally 1,800 acres, the area under cultivation grew as Disston, whether by guess or inside knowledge, believed a two penny per pound bounty was about to be passed by the Congress. Cuba, at the time, had lost the low-cost advantage of slave labor and the price of sugar on the world market was increasing dramatically. To satisfy growing demand in 1890, and to encourage domestic production, the bounty passed.

Disston later invested another $1 million in the plantation and brought new northern partners into his operation incorporated as the American Sugar Manufacturing Corporation. The very nomenclature indicates a move away from the agrarian history and traditions of growing sugarcane, and into the new world of management consultants, automation and techniques of mass production.

A financial panic gripped the United States in 1893 and in 1894, Congress rescinded the sugar bounty. Following the financial disaster, hard freezes in the winters of 1894 and 1895 throttled the agricultural industries of Florida and chilled Disston's interest in pursuing his Florida dreams. In April 1896, he took his own life.

The saga of Hamilton Disston would be repeated over and over in Florida. It was to become a land of boundless opportunity pursued by unscrupulous speculators always betting on the next deal to be made, with unlimited riches to be had almost immediately. It represented the coming of the Gilded Age, when American would see massive income disparity, and when sugar production would become a central issue with the outbreak of hostilities in the Spanish-American War.

Beet sugar growers in the Plains and Upper Midwest, along with cane sugar from Louisiana, were producing about 275,000 tons each year, but it was inadequate to satisfy the sweet tooth of the American consumer. By 1900, annual demand for sugar amounted to six million tons worldwide and nearly two million tons in the United States. The U.S. had a mere seventy-six million souls at the time, representing 5% of the world's population but consuming one-third of the world's sugar.

With the Spanish chased out of Cuba and the Philippines, the United States was gaining the capacity to grow and refine large amounts of sugar to compete with beet production in Europe. But it was not nearly enough to satisfy demand, so the industry, while investing heavily in Cuba, began to look at the State of Florida. The two major commodities after the Civil War were cotton and lumber. But cotton had to contend with a little pest called the boll weevil and the timber industry depended upon long time horizons to grow and cut trees at a sustainable level.

RUFUS ROSE

The Florida state chemist at the turn of the century was a gent named Rufus Rose. A former Louisiana riverboat captain and successful political figure in central Florida, he was convinced that sugar could be grown in Florida in massive amounts over multiple ratoons. Rose was trained as an engineer and understood, from his years in Louisiana, how to grow sugarcane. Headquartered at the Okeechobee Land and Drainage Company offices in Kissimmee City, which he had laid out in 1883, he began to grow cane on the St. Cloud Plantation in 1886 after creating a drainage system for the fields using the Kissimmee River as a source for water. Growing sugarcane, rice and corn, Disston became interested and Rose sold him a half-interest in the operation.

With Disston's financial backing, a refining operation was added and the area cultivated expanded to 1,800 acres. "None but first-class sugar was made," and the yield was "superior to any American record up to that time," Rose commented in his book.[12]

With the two-cent bounty from the McKinley tariff of 1890, the business was comfortably profitable. After Disston's initial vision was brought to reality by a second $1 million investment and expansion to 36,000 acres capable of producing two hundred tons of refined sugar each day, he pressed even harder to expand. But Rose became uncomfortable with what he regarded as Disston's rampant speculation attended by badly managed growth and sold his half-interest back to his partner.

Interest in Disston's experiment had reached Washington D.C. in 1891 with the chief chemist of the present-day United States Department of Agriculture, but without Rose's knowledge and guidance, St. Cloud fell quickly into disrepair. The canals and irrigation system became clogged with weeds and the Panic of 1893 brought the financial system, and Disston, to ruin.

Meanwhile Rose had moved on to become state chemist for Florida and continued to press for development of cane plantations south of Lake Okeechobee. In 1903, at the first meeting of the Interstate Sugar Cane Growers Association (ISCGA), he described how his experience in the muck at St. Cloud, amplified by his knowledge of the availability of water from the Kissimmee and Caloosahatchee Rivers, and the rich soils south of Lake Okeechobee, could create the perfect environment for cultivation of sugar plants. While acknowledging the halting experiments in the north and central parts of the state, it was the first instance of a large-scale example of how south Florida, below the Kissimmee Lakes area, was the best place to grow sugarcane.

In her magnificent book, *Raising Cane in the Glades*, author Gail Hollander traces the meetings of the ISCGA from 1903 to 1906, and details how members from Florida came to realize that the state's future lay in its ability to grow, process and refine granulated sugar similar to that produced by beets in the northern states (which was supplying most of the granulated sugar consumed in America). In addition, she points out that the Florida contingent was convinced there was a ready market for raw sugar in refineries located near the fields while syrup, easier to process into a final product, was harder to sell, and that a horizontally integrated growing, processing and refining system was desirable for financial success.[13]

Rose's expansive vision was for a sugar cane belt, such as exists today, along the southern tier of states with refineries nearby and transportation to markets readily available through the rivers and canals feeding into the Gulf of Mexico. His work was known and supported by

Governor Napoleon Bonaparte Broward who, in his 1904 campaign, promised to drain the Everglades to make the land available for agriculture, notably sugarcane.

Broward addressed the 1906 ISCGA conference, proclaiming that the area south of Lake Okeechobee was ideal with the longest growing season and perfect soil, dismissing the idea of a cane belt in other southern states since his administration would zealously drain enough land, three million acres, to satisfy domestic demand for granulated sugar. In his remarks, he also pooh-poohed the Jeffersonian idea of small farmers, saying that they would be satisfied with just growing plants whereas his vision was for vertically integrated operations from growing to refining—very much along the lines of the current model for the sugar industry in south Florida.

The period between the turn of the century and the war was marked by a growing awareness of the value of drained land in Florida, notably the area south of Lake Okeechobee. It marked a turning point from the reality of small and scattered sugar farming throughout the state into a larger vision of massive acreage and integrated operations to produce millions of tons of sugar a year. It changed the way leaders in the state regarded south Florida, no longer a frontier guarded by mosquitoes and alligators but rather with sugar as the defining centrality of an economic engine in a state of limited natural resources save two—sunshine and the Everglades.

NAPOLEON BONAPARTE BROWARD

Broward was the first to openly propose state financing of Everglades drainage. He was a large man, another former riverboat captain, smuggler of arms and men into Cuba to support the revolution before the Spanish-American War and a member of the liberal wing of the Democratic Party. Given little chance of winning the governorship, he campaigned up and down the state in small towns and rural areas with his primary message being what he called the "Empire of the Everglades."

After winning the election with a tiny margin, Broward immediately turned his attention to draining the Everglades, beginning with surveys and looking toward a master plan for managing the water in the southern quarter of a state that received an average of fifty-five inches of rainfall each year. His choice for oversight of the project was J. O. Wright.

The one major difference between Disston's drainage project and Broward's was the financing. Whereas Disston was using his own money, and looking for a quick return of capital, Broward took a long view and relied upon taxation to the chagrin of many Floridians. He was pilloried in the press for his acreage tax but remained unfazed and committed.

Word spread quickly, all the way to Washington, where Broward's drainage project was lionized. President Theodore Roosevelt decided to pay a visit to see first-hand how the project was proceeding. He declared it to be a fine example of drainage and, despite his usual policy of conserving natural areas, encouraged Broward to press forward. Roosevelt saw no redeeming features to the Everglades, preferring it to be forever altered to serve the needs and wants of Floridians.

But Broward's grand plan was frustrated when the acreage tax was nullified by a court decision, and he was hard-pressed to continue. His answer was what other Florida governors had done to finance projects: sell state lands. In this case, Broward found Richard Bolles, a hungry real estate developer from Colorado, willing to buy 508,000 acres for $1 million. Payment would take place over time, at $150,000 per year for the first three years. Bolles' first interest was in development but lacking in any part of the discussions while negotiating the deal was J. O. Wright's survey and engineer's report.[14]

A version of the report was released in 1910 but quickly edited as many of Wright's assumptions were questioned, particularly his assumption that drainage could be done quickly, at low cost with canals alone and with no need for a protective dike around Lake Okeechobee.

Wright's error was simply explained. He had designed his canals to hold much less water than fell during Florida's rainy, wet season from May to November. Yet speculation ruled the day and only a few souls publicly objected to the land boom taking place in south Florida. One of those objectors was Frank Stoneman, editor of the *Miami News-Record*, and father of the more famous family member,

Marjory Stoneman Douglas, author of the classic book *The Everglades: River of Grass.*

Wright's unofficial draft report was widely circulated and widely amended by real estate speculators to the point where uncertainty existed as to which copy was the genuine article. Amid the hue and cry, the U.S. House of Representatives investigated why a report, authorized and paid for by taxpayer dollars, had never been formally approved and released. With all the pressure, Wright resigned from the drainage project, but then produced a document titled *The Everglades of Florida: Their Adaptability for the Growth of Sugar Cane.* Published in 1912, Wright identified himself on the cover of his white paper as "...formerly Supervising Drainage Engineer in the United States Department of Agriculture and later Chief Drainage Engineer for the State of Florida." [15]

Published in Tallahassee and harkening back to the 1891 USDA report by Harvey Wiley, a glowing assessment came from Wright's pen:

> "Although sugar cane may not yield as large a return per acre as some vegetables that are now grown, it is practically a sure crop. Where the conditions are at all favorable a total failure of a cane crop is unknown. With adequate provisions for controlling the water the growing of sugar cane in the Everglades is less hazardous than any other branch of agriculture. It is probably freer from disease than any other

staple crop produced in the United States. It requires no special skill in planting and cultivation; it will produce a profitable crop for five to eight years without replanting. In fact, sugar cane is the ideal staple crop to be grown in the Everglades." [16]

He concluded his report with the comment: "South Florida will no longer be spoken of as the 'rich man's playground' but it will actually become the greatest wealth producing section of the United States." [17]

Wright estimated that two million acres could be drained and, once planted, would produce $180 million a year in revenue—equal to the total assessed value of property in the entire state at that time. While this appeared to justify much of his prior work, the emphasis on agriculture, rather than development, undercut the real estate speculation but only briefly.

Disston had purchased four million acres in 1881 for twenty-five cents per acre; Bolles had paid fifty cents per acre. But by the time Broward died in 1910, land was selling at retail for fifteen dollars an acre. Because drainage was proceeding apace, Henry Flagler was making plans to run his railroad through reclaimed areas and the promise of Florida's future, whether in sugar or rooftops, lay in reclaimed muck.

WORLD WAR I

With the tiger's tail tweaked, there was no turning back, and during the period between the turn of the century and the entry of the United States into the war, drainage activity occurred in fits and starts, boosted and financed by anxious politicians and speculators chasing a quick buck.

By 1912, word had gotten out that the drainage was not only failing but, in some areas, actually contributed to flooding. The "Empire of the Everglades" promoted by Broward was jeopardized by large investors threatening to pull out and bankrupting the IIF yet another time. While all the promotion had been for small parcels, ten acres each, major investors told Governor Gilchrist that to save the project the focus needed to be on larger agricultural operations, not small retail parcels, and sugarcane growing was at the top of mind.

The governor's solution was to issue state-backed bonds to finance drainage. The work would be overseen by a New York Engineering firm chosen carefully to satisfy investors. An oversight commission appointed by the company would be headed by Isham Randolph who had earned his chops, by overseeing the Chicago drainage system and served at the pleasure of President Roosevelt as a member of the Panama Canal Commission.

Once convened, the commission's report proposed an entirely different approach to the earlier method of draining the land incrementally, but to do it on a massive scale much as Disston had originally proposed.

> "Our conclusion, based upon our study of ascertained facts, is that drainage of the Florida Everglades is entirely practicable and can be accomplished at a cost which the value of the reclaimed land will justify, the cost per acre being very small." [18]

The report stimulated interest among investors who had shied away from Gilchrist's state-backed bonds and Broward's campaign-based optimism as to the future of the drained land. To promote the new paradigm of massive corporate farming operations, the Southern States Land and Timber Company (SSLTC) was formed to purchase Disston's land in 1915 for the same price he paid: 25¢ per acre.

The initial money came from New York and management came from the Burguières family from Louisiana, bringing with it the seeds and technology of growing cane along the northern Gulf coast. Eventually, the J. M. Burguières Company of Louisiana would buy SSLTC and would play a major role in development of Florida's sugar industry. What is particularly notable is that the company began operations during the second year of a world war, with the advantage of worldwide shortages of sugar as beet growing areas of Europe were forced out of production. The wholesale price of most commodities was rising; sugar was moving up as much as 20% per year. One of the reasons was that industrial alcohol was a critical ingredient in the manufacture of munitions and an adequate supply was necessary in the war effort. British scientists had found, just prior to World War I, that acetone, necessary to the gelatinization of cordite, could be fermented from molasses. And cordite was critical as a propellant for large guns used by the Allied navy, artillery and tanks corps.

Before the assassination of the archduke, Germany was Europe's largest beet sugar producer and as hostilities on the continent spread, supply dwindled, pushing the world price up. In 1914, European production amounted to 8,217,000 tons; by 1918 the crop yield amounted to 3,422,000 tons. Russia, beset by both the war and revolution was hardest hit, losing 95% of its beet sugar production.[19]

When the United Sates entered the war in 1917, it created the U.S. Sugar Equalization Board in July and quickly put in a controlled price ceiling of seven cents per pound wholesale. But when the war ended, price controls and related import quotas were cancelled and the free market was allowed to operate, creating a price bubble in sugar during an eighteen-month period that led to a feeding frenzy called the Dance of the Millions.

The price of a pound of sugar went up 80% from 1914 to 1918 with the primary beneficiary of reduced supply and increased price being Cuba, which became the world's largest producer, going from 2,598,000 tons to 3,972,000 tons.[20]

Cuba's increased production during the four years of the war became an irresistible opportunity for investors. The cessation of hostilities in 1918 created a speculative bubble with the world price nearly tripling by May of 1920. But, as typical with any commodity bubble, the market quickly normalized as European beet sugar came back onto the market, and the price dropped eighteen months later, to about five cents per pound. In lock-step with prices, the cost of land in Cuba shot up proportionally, and as the bubble burst, American banks quickly foreclosed on loans and took possession of Cuban property, establishing a large foreign presence on the island. The story of the bubble eventually had a significant effect on development of the sugar industry in Florida, so it's worth telling in greater detail.

THE DANCE OF THE MILLIONS

The world war and the demand for molasses was the prelude to the 'Dance' which was about to make Cuba a very wealthy country in a very short period of time. As the money flowed in and to display newly found wealth, neighborhoods like Miramar and the Vedado in Havana were developed with spacious houses and a stunning variety of architecture. A large part of the opulence was from newly minted money from *colonos*, where large tracts of land were purchased, mostly on credit, to encourage transformation of raw and grazing land into cane fields. The *colonos* grew exponentially to over fifty thousand families, during the five years of the war.

American capital flowed into the country too, financing purchase of land and the creation of new *centrales* based on a business model where large mills, fed by the *colonos'* harvest, operated at maximum pressing capacity, squeezing farmers by setting the price they would pay for harvested plants.

The older model, of *ingenios,* had become out of date. The *ingenios* was centralization of business and dwellings surrounding a water-driven mill combining a business model with modest social amenities where the workers would be immediately available during both the harvest and growing seasons. The *centrale* was larger and more mechanized and relied upon a system of subcontractors, as well as former *ingenios* converted into *colonos.* With the conversion to *centrales* in Cuba, the business became semi-oligarchic in terms of pricing power.

Over two-dozen new *centrales* were created during the war years, and investment in Cuban sugar paid off handsomely as world price rose steadily, until the advent of price controls which quickly skimmed the froth off the market with a firm price set by the American Sugar Equalization Board.

The total value of exports from Cuba amounted to $175 million (in 1913 dollars) growing to $580 million by 1919. Sugar was by far the largest component going from $125 million to $510 million or 88% of all exports that year.[21]

Once controls were lifted, the price increased even though European beet sugar came back on the market more quickly than expected escalating from 6½¢ in September 1919 to 22½¢ in May 1920—a stunning increase. The Dance of the Millions was in full swing.

In July 1919, the Cuban Commission, consisting of three men appointed by Cuba's president, had written the American Sugar Equalization Board suggesting that it might consider buying the entire 1919-1920 harvest. The price, 6½¢, was fractionally higher than the 1918-1919 price. The concern in Cuba was that with unrestrained post-war market conditions, wild price fluctuations would continue and a hedge would be preferable to relying upon the daily vagaries of commodity prices.

In addition, the U.S. had ratified Prohibition in January 1919. While alcoholic beverages declined somewhat, sugar-laden soft drinks doubled from eighteen bottles per person in 1914 to over thirty-eight bottles in 1919, but the legal processing of molasses for rum was severely curtailed.

The same month Prohibition went into effect, Java began to sell raw sugar on the world market at 11¢ per pound. Cuban *centrales* and major landholders anticipated fantastic profits. At the time, the United States and Britain accounted for nearly two-thirds of the export surplus in the world market and there remained only a vague hope that a deal could be struck to keep the Cuban supply chain to those two countries moving at a fair and fixed, negotiated price, despite the roiling market.

But by September, a portion of the Cuban crop had been sold on the open market at 11¢ and enthusiasm for an agreement quickly faded as the price moved up. American producers, waiting for an agreement, deferred purchase contracts and by December, the price had risen to 12¢ per pound. The *colonos* were aware of the escalation and began to withhold the harvest in the middle of the *zafra*—that period from September to February when cane plants are cut and sent for processing. Strikes and supply issues had slowed shipments in early 1920. There was a concern that the harvest was reduced by unfavorable weather during the growing season and, as the mills began to crank up to full output so did prices, peaking at 22½¢ per pound by May 1920 caused by frenzied bidding by refiners. The 1919-1920 crop was valued at $999 million as against $510 million for the 1918-1919 crop.

But then the bubble, against which millions of dollars in loans were made, burst. Domestic refiners in both the U.S. and Britain refused to pay the exorbitant prices, demand began to drop, and other sources began to export heavily to the United States, creating an additional 500,000 tons of supply and driving the price down to 4½¢ per pound by 1920 year-end.

Cuban financial institutions, having loaned heavily during the peak of Dance of the Millions, were caught short and a banking panic hit the island like a hurricane. Local banks were subject to runs by depositors with people flooding the streets of Havana to withdraw their savings, forcing five of the largest banks to immediately slam their doors. At the end of the carnage, twenty Cuban banks had collapsed and foreign money was able to move in to take advantage of the carnage. In the end, 18,000 *colonos* lost their land.

The results of the burst bubble radically altered the ownership structure of Cuban sugar. As an example, National City Bank of New York in March 1921, as trustee, brought to market a financing of the Cuban-American Sugar Company for $10 million in mortgage collateral bonds with an 8% coupon, sporting eleven mills all either bought out of foreclosure or taken as collateral against unpaid debts. American investment in Cuba in 1911 was $205 million; by 1924 it was $1.2 billion.[22]

The price stabilized at 3.75¢ per pound after the 'Dance.' The amount was higher than that of the period between 1885 and 1914 so the Cuban economy, while painfully damaged, was able to survive due to its low-cost structure.[23]

Florida—Four Case Studies

It was only after World War I that the State of Florida began starting on a definite path to become the largest sugar-producing region in the country. It was a time when large, well-financed companies run by entrepreneurs, were supported by state and federal government research facilities studying soils, fertilizers and hybridized cane plants The period leading up to the Great Depression was marked by a few notable experiments, some of which failed taking investors down with them, but leaving a legacy of experience and knowledge that proved invaluable to the future of growing and harvesting sugarcane in the Everglades.

The St. Cloud Plantation and Hamilton Disston, already covered, was an early example of the complexities of growing cane in the muck around Lake Okeechobee. Other companies would follow having not been seriously misled by consultants about the efficacy and fertility of south

Florida soils and by the vagaries of weather. They came in with eyes wide open. Aside from issues of agronomy and mechanization, these projects all represented Florida's version of an innovative concept begun in Cuba and Louisiana: vertical integration of the growing, harvesting, processing and refining of sugar.

SOUTHERN STATES LAND AND TIMBER (SSLTC)

The SSLTC had been organized in 1902 in New York by two members of the Lehman family, both grandsons of Herbert Lehman of the mercantile bank in his name. The company had acquired two million acres around Lake Okeechobee and had joined forces with railroad magnate Henry Flagler and other landowners to promote drainage. The land was the same ground once owned by the St. Cloud Plantation. It had been purchased from the family of Hamilton Disston which had no interest in pursuing agriculture in Florida.

Over time, Southern States used real estate sales to finance many of their operations. While ostensibly sold for either farming or as smaller parcels for houses, the investors knew that railroad right of way paved the path for development as Flagler had proved when, during the Gilded Age, he built the Florida East Coast Railway and to satisfy tourists using his passenger trains, great edifices that survive to this day including the Breakers and Royal Poinciana Hotels in Palm Beach and the Ponce de Leon Hotel in St. Augustine.

Southern States management was influential in the corridors of power in Washington and Tallahassee, as the company aggressively pursued drainage with lawsuits against the Internal Improvement Fund and pursuit of federal support. Rewarded for its effort, one million acres was reclaimed with completion of the C-51, or Palm Beach Canal, in 1917.

By that time, the Burguières interests had gained control of Southern States. Led by Jules Burguières, Sr., the family had been growing sugarcane in Louisiana since 1871 as the market picked up after the Civil War. Intrigued by opportunities in Cuba at the turn of the century, they purchased a small amount of land in Matanzas province in 1909 but did nothing for four years, until the beginning of World War I.

His son, Jules Burguières, Jr., went to Cuba in 1913 with the New York-based Cuban-American Sugar Company which, at the time, controlled a half million acres on the island and was into both processing and rum distilling. He left the following year, sensing an overwhelming opportunity in Florida with his family's over forty years of experience in growing and processing cane in Louisiana.

However, in the back of every investor's mind, including Southern States' management at the time, was the land mini-boom spreading over south Florida. Ads run in newspapers throughout the country offered land originally purchased for twenty-five cents an acre for anywhere from ten to fifty dollars, but with all the drainage problems much of the land was virtually worthless, giving rise to one of the most oft-repeated tropes in south Florida: "I have bought land by the acre, I have bought land by the foot; but, by God, I have never before bought land by the gallon." [24]

During this time, the company was experimenting with various crops because the soil, while generally rich in nutrients like nitrogen, lacked phosphate and potash and tended to be somewhat acidic. As time passed the company's operations provided valuable information on proper combinations of fertilization, but the underlying interest was on land sales and development.

Flagler's railroad ran down the coast, but SSLTC knew that it needed rail service inland to make its holdings more attractive for development. So, in 1924, the company sold 100,000 acres for $1.5 million to the Seaboard Railroad, whose tracks eventually ran from central Florida down to Palm Beach and Miami. Earlier, the company had sold 610,000 acres to advertising executive Barron Collier, who later became Florida's largest landholder and incorporator of the county that bears his name today.

Southern States survives having retained mineral rights to much of the land it sold over the years. It was merged into the J. M. Burguières Company, headquartered in Louisiana, around 2001. It contributed to the growing body of knowledge as to the right combination of seed and fertilizer to grow sugarcane in the Everglades, but more importantly provided an example of the ease with which land originally thought to grow crops could eventually grow rooftops.

PENNSUCO

Attracted by the two financial opportunities of real estate development and growing sugarcane with a lack of environmental regulation and the easy exploitation of workers, the Pennsylvania Sugar Company, better known as Pennsuco, was licensed to do business in Florida in November 1919. The company's management in Philadelphia became interested in the Everglades through the persistence of a large landowner, B. B. Tatum, and entered into protracted and difficult negotiations for a lease and purchase agreement of 70,000 acres in western Miami-Dade County. The lease was for $1.95 per acre with a purchase option at $12 per acre if the land proved productive. If not, the Tatum Company would refund lease payments.

Pennsuco's interest in growing sugarcane in south Florida was heightened during the negotiations with Tatum by a visit to the United States by Cuba's second president, Juan Miguel Gomez. A general in the war against Spain, Gomez had been elected in 1908 and was a popular figure in the country during his first years in office. But he had a dark side manifest in 1912 when, running for re-election, he declared martial law and massacred a large group of Afro-Cubans who were protesting a law prohibiting race or religion to determine political affiliation. Beaten in the election, he then used his political connections to enrich himself and frequently visit the United States.

While in the U.S. in 1919, he toured the Everglades and pronounced the land unsuitable for the cultivation of sugar, unless major changes to drainage and fertilization were made. Gomez's opinion was highly respected, and the negotiations were slowed by Pennsuco until the company, after further investigation, decided that Gomez's purpose may have been to protect Cuban sugar interests from Florida competition as the Dance of the Millions was just beginning.

Pennsuco was committed to mechanization of the sugarcane harvest. Up until that time, harvest took place during the *zafra*—that time when cane plants were ripe. Hand cutting of the stalks, known as being "on the knife," had been done by slave labor, then by low-wage free blacks, and finally by migrant workers. But the cost of human labor, with attendant issues such as availability in adequate numbers and the need for nearby housing, encouraged the company to seek other means of both planting and cutting the cane. The company's thinking at the time was that mechanization could be easily introduced into Florida because it believed (mistakenly) that that the cane fields had been drained and the soil dried out sufficiently to allow machines to operate with impunity.

While the machinery, using a Ford Model T chassis with wide-rimmed wheels and tires, was conceptually sound, the heavy machines often sunk into the muck where drainage was poorly engineered and bogged down as the summer rains kept the soil soggy at the beginning of the harvest season.

Soil in the Everglades was unlike that found in Louisiana and the transference of knowledge was limited. Pennsuco's operation was helped by the establishment of a United States Department of Agriculture (USDA) research station at Canal Point, on the southern edge of Lake Okeechobee, in 1920. The station bred hundreds of different sugarcane cultivars searching for disease resistance and high saccharin yield through both hybridization and combinations of chemical fertilizers that would enrich Florida's muck. Significantly, cane plants grown in south Florida's tropical climate were able to flower, so the research station over the years was also able to distribute seeds worldwide for germination.

The station, just after beginning operations, was immediately frustrated by a frost in December despite assurances that the Everglades, protected by its location south of the lake, would never reach temperatures low enough to kill sugarcane plants. While that was true, cane grown a short distance from the lake was severely affected.

The Florida legislature expressed its support of biological research for the nascent sugarcane industry by funding a State of Florida facility at Belle Glade on the Hillsborough Canal in Palm Beach County. Research there had focus on a variety of crops, and while its experiments with soil nutrients would prove valuable for cane growing operations, it would be eventually disastrous for the environment.

The Pennsuco experiment was a partial success because in using hybrids from Canal Point research it showed mosaic could be eliminated in the Everglades, but ultimately failed because the drainage promised by the Internal Improvement Fund, and guided by the Wright report, was never completed. But in failing it also offered guidance as to how, and how not to, mechanize the planting and harvest of sugarcane.

SOUTHERN SUGAR COMPANY AND CELOTEX

What was becoming apparent was that many of the companies involved in sugar operations in the Everglades had interlocking directorates and connections that cemented relationships with financial institutions as well. One of the prime lenders was National City Bank of New York whose officers held board seats on multiple corporations doing business in the Everglades, mainly for the purpose of overseeing and protecting the bank's investments.

Social and political connections were equally important. The Cape Sable Club of which Jules Burguières, Jr., was a member also had William Jennings Bryan on its roster, and at the Everglades Club in Palm Beach, Burguières broke bread with the head of one of Louisiana's most celebrated corporations at the time and, for a few years, owner of the ill-fated Southern Sugar Company.

The Southern Sugar Company was organized in 1925 by Bror Dahlberg. He owned the Celotex Company in Marrero, Louisiana which made a form of insulating board used in construction based on bagasse, the stalk and leaf remains of a sugarcane plant after squeezing out the sucrose and other liquids. Its qualities were superior in all types of climate and orders had soared to hundreds of millions of feet. By 1925, it was the largest manufacturer of insulating board in the world. But there was one problem in meeting the booming demand. Louisiana was not meeting Celotex's needs. The company was importing 60% of its bagasse from Cuba with heavy freight charges.

Louisiana cane plants were suffering from mosaic disease, and the annual yield was declining, so Dahlberg hired a team of agronomists who found a hybrid plant in Java which, combined with a Himalayan variety, seemed to do well in Louisiana. Known as the P.O.J. hybrid, sucrose yield increased dramatically. Dahlberg had solved an immediate problem, and in doing so became interested in the business and the potential for profit in growing sugarcane. And the next best place to do that was Florida's Everglades.

Flush with success from the new hybrid, Dahlberg hired the Smith and Ames Company to assay the muck south of Lake Okeechobee. The report back was glowing and optimistic:

"... the important element nitrogen is present in twenty times the necessary amount and phosphoric acid over three times what is required. Potash, however, is somewhat lacking in quantity, as analyses show only about 0.12% instead of the 0.25% considered useful for the best growth of cane. For maximum results the amount lacking will possibly have to be supplied artificially, at small expense."[25]

The report went on to estimate a yield of forty tons per acre, a staggering amount when compared to Cuba's average yield of twenty tons. Adding to support for cane operations in south Florida, the Canal Point research station had grown a pilot crop of sugarcane at nearly fifty tons per acre.

Dahlberg was convinced, and by 1926 his company was clearing over 35,000 acres for sugarcane cultivation. But the Smith and Ames report ended up being a dud. There was not enough phosphorous for maximum cane growth and the amount of potash needed was seriously underestimated. These factors could be overcome by heavy fertilization at no small expense, but that same year ended up with a disastrous event for the lands and fragile environmental infrastructure south of Lake Okeechobee—for a reason unrelated to soil quality.

The Great Miami Hurricane made landfall on Florida's east coast in September. Driving inland, it breached earthen dikes around Lake Okeechobee. The storm surge wiped out Clewiston and submerged Moore Haven under fifteen feet of water. It was estimated that over 300 people were killed by the storm; many bodies were never found. It would be the worst hurricane to hit Florida, in terms of property damage, until Wilma in 2005.

Clewiston was hardest hit. It was a planned community, platted in 1920 to integrate multiple social and public facilities reminiscent of the Chautauqua style, promoted by easy access to passengers through the terminal of the Atlantic Coast Line Railroad.

Despite the hurricane, Dahlberg decided to proceed with both land drainage and planting sugarcane to become the dominant sugar producer in Florida, convincing his friend, Jules Burguières, Jr., to handle operations in West Palm Beach and Clewiston where he built the Clewiston Sugar House. Opening in 1928, the mill was capable of grinding 1,500 tons a day; a second mill was planned at Canal Point with a capacity of 2,500 tons a day.

Once again, in the midst of constructing mills and digging drainage ditches, another hurricane hit south Florida, this time even more deadly. The 1928 Okeechobee Hurricane blew through two years later, again in September. That storm, with gusts over 162 mph, killed over 2,500 people. As the rear eyewall passed over Lake Okeechobee, all dikes failed and with a storm surge of over twenty feet, the towns of Pahokee, Canal Point and Belle Glade, where the USDA and state research stations were located, were literally washed off the map.

To add to the accelerating woes of the decade, the stock market crashed in October 1929 and south Florida was overwhelmed with an invasion of fruit flies that decimated row crops and chased tourists back north.

After the 1930-1931 harvest, Dahlberg's Southern Sugar Company failed and was forced into bankruptcy. It was acquired by creditors, most notably Charles S. Mott, a vice president and founder of General Motors Corporation and Clarence Bitting, a financier who became president of the renamed U.S. Sugar Corporation. Bitting, from New York, was a good communicator and comfortable walking the halls of Congress which led to legislation highly favorable to the domestic sugar companies, most notably the one that he ran. The Mott ownership would continue uninterrupted to the present day.

FELLSMERE

The story of Fellsmere Farms is one that demonstrated the rising level of interest and activity sponsored by the relentless boosterism of Governor Broward. It is also a tale of the origins of one of the most important trade names of the refined sugar in the United States—Florida Crystals.

The town was founded in 1911 when Nelson Fell bought 18,000 acres in what was then St. Lucie County (now Indian River County). Fell, heir to a large British mining company, had made a fortune extracting copper in Russia and was planning to retire to his family's plantation in Virginia at age fifty-two. He visited Kissimmee to see his friend, Captain Rufus Rose, the man who had acted as real estate agent for Hamilton Disston. The town, named eponymously, was the first in the South to allow women to vote when in June 1915 Zena Dreir cast a ballot in a race for City Council of the newly built, and rapidly growing, town of Fellsmere.

Fell, with big money from a Virginia engineer named Oscar Crosby, began dredging land around the town using gravity as the only means of draining and irrigating the fields of Fellsmere Farm Company, located near the east coast of Florida north of Lake Okeechobee. The level of activity, combined with Governor Broward's proclaiming the "Empire of the Everglades," attracted farmers from throughout the country, among them a twenty-one-year-old named Frank Heiser from Indiana.

Gritty and determined, Heiser cleared twenty acres for row crops, but found the market for tomatoes and peppers saturated, so he lost money and shifted to citrus. Success depended heavily upon the drainage system, but as with J. O. Wright, the quantity of water dumped on Florida was underestimated.

No one understood the danger created by inadequate drainage until July 1915 when heavy rains flooded the City of Fellsmere and surrounding fields. The town during the rainy season found its streets flooded into unwanted canals. It was said that if folks wanted to find Fellsmere, they would know "when they were knee deep in water." [26]

It was reported that some residents left by boat.

After the disaster, outside capital dried up and the commencement of war forced the farming operation to default on loans and file for bankruptcy. The reorganized company was rebranded as Fellsmere Farms in 1918, with Frank Heiser as corporate secretary.

Heiser was always convinced that the future of Fellsmere Farms was in growing and processing sugarcane. In pursuit of that goal, he organized the Fellsmere Sugar Association, consisting of a small group of farmers, to experiment with various combinations of hybrids and fertilizers, and to finance a small grinding operation. The local newspaper, Fellsmere Tribune, was a strong advocate for Heiser's plan but things began to fall apart in 1922 when the local bank fell upon hard times. Never one to give up, Heiser reorganized as the Standard Agricultural Chemical Company, two years later called the Ammoniate Products Company, to dry and grind Fellsmere muck as a stabilizer for fertilizers. The company lasted for about two years.

But Heiser was still fascinated with sugarcane and by 1929 was able to produce a sizable crop on a hundred-acre plot. He realized that success was a matter of scale, and that smaller experimental plots would not provide an economic basis for sustainable growing and processing. To reach the right size he needed at least one million dollars going right into the first year of the Great Depression. To buttress his argument with New York investors, he got testimony from supervisors at the Fellsmere Drainage District, which he had formed in 1918 and was still executive director. But Heiser's reputation followed him to New York, with a history of failed companies and loss of capital.

Relentlessly promoting high potential returns from a properly scaled sugar operation by the Fellsmere Sugar Company, he finally convinced four investors to come in; two of them had experience in Cuba.

Operating on a shoestring, and after clearing 1,000 acres, Heiser built a Rube Goldberg mill out of used parts from plants closed in Louisiana and Florida, completing the work in 1932. By harvest time beginning in November, seven hundred acres were ready for cutting with another seven hundred being cleared. By April 1933, the grinding produced two million pounds of raw sugar. The company was doing well and residents were delighted to have jobs, even at sixteen cents per hour, when the national unemployment rate exceeded twenty-five per cent.

But there were two storm clouds on the horizon, one from the west coast of Africa. The first storm hit Florida's Treasure Coast in early September 1933 at Jupiter Island with 125 mph winds. It was one of the most active hurricane seasons in history. Rolling across the state, it tore the roof off the Fellsmere mill and inundated sugarcane fields with up to ten inches of rain, causing a reduction in the sugar content of the plants. Despite the storm, 2.8 million pounds of raw sugar were processed.

Flush with success, the Fellsmere Sugar Company

expected a bumper crop in 1934. It had built dormitory space for four hundred Caribbean guest workers to perform the back-breaking work of cutting cane plants, but in December temperatures dropped precipitously throughout Florida. Fellsmere's weather station reported a low of nineteen degrees.[27] Heiser's four investors were terrified. One dropped out but the cane cutting went on twenty-four hours a day and the final yield of raw sugar, due to fast work and increased acreage, was up eight per cent from the prior year. In addition, the federal government, having been granted the power to mandate acreage limitations and marketing allotments for agricultural products by the Agricultural Adjustment Act of 1933 and Jones-Costigan Act of 1934, decided to not issue quotas for 1935. Given the situation, Heiser decided to build a sugar refining plant, a questionable investment in the midst of the deepening Depression.

To accomplish this, Heiser turned the Fellsmere Sugar Company into a cooperative—Fellsmere Sugar Producers Association—separating growing operations from grinding and refining. To raise the million dollars he needed, Heiser obtained a government loan, his three remaining investors chipped in, and he put every bit of his remaining capital into building the first refinery in Florida—capable of producing over one hundred tons a day of finished granulated sugar, using the trade name Florida Crystals. By the end of the Depression, it was selling over 5.5 million pounds of white sugar.

But before the Depression ended, the Secretary of Agriculture put into effect quotas under the Jones-Costigan Act, sending Heiser and Clarence Bitting of the United States Sugar Company to Washington to plead the case for Florida against both cane growers in Louisiana and beet farmers in the upper West and Midwest.

After a series of ups and downs, World War II began and created massive labor shortages of men willing to work in the cane fields. In addition, the government was asserting greater control of production. Despite the best efforts by Washington to seek stability, the price of sugar dropped, and in 1943, Heiser and his investors decided to sell the cooperative and all its assets to a Puerto Rican syndicate.

The story of Fellsmere is important for three reasons. First, it showed that growing sugarcane in central Florida north of Lake Okeechobee was always a risky business, obvious since the New Smyrna colony. Land south of the Fellsmere area was preferable because as cold fronts swept the state from the northwest, the warm waters of the lake would ameliorate ambient temperatures. Second, it was really the first instance in the United States which showed that all operations properly scaled, from planting to marketing a finished consumer product, was the preferred business model. And third, given the sputtering start of Nelson Fell's idea, it showed that the drainage of water, repeated in the case of Hamilton Disston, Bror Dahlberg and other pioneers, was the single most important factor in building a sustainable agricultural operation in Florida's Everglades.

U.S. on the World Stage

During the period between the beginning of World War I and the Great Depression, while Pennsuco and Dahlberg were draining the Everglades and experimenting with growing sugar, the United States was in the enviable position of having its full productive capacity in both manufacturing and agriculture untouched by the ravages of war. European allies had borrowed heavily from American bankers to finance the conflict, the continent was devastated, and the U.S. had replaced Great Britain as the preeminent world power. The Jazz Age was in full swing and, reminiscent of the Gilded Age at the turn of the century, outrageous profits and economic inequality were once again being celebrated as great examples of the American Way of Life and the just rewards of unrestrained capitalism.

But Europe came back more quickly than expected, and American business and agriculture saw their ability to raise prices and control world markets eroding, leading to fits and starts of protectionist policies. The main vehicle was the tariff. Having gained attention early in the Theodore Roosevelt administration, and divided by party lines with Republicans generally protectionist and Democrats known as free traders, tariffs moved up and down for the next twenty years, depending upon the political party in power.

TARIFFS HEAT UP

The 1921 Act was followed by the Fordney-McCumber Act of 1922, a broad tariff act, which boosted the tax on Cuban sugar from 1.6¢ per pound to 1.76¢ per pound. But sugar was a prickly commodity to deal with in the Congress. Duty-free supply sources, U.S. territories such as Hawaii and the Philippines and Puerto Rico, while having no seats in the House or Senate, had powerful and influential friends such as the huge Spreckels operation with plantations in Hawaii and refining plants in California. All argued they needed to be protected because Cuba remained the largest and lowest cost producer of raw sugar in the western hemisphere, supplying 65% of raw sugar to the U.S. market in 1922.[28] This would play out during the coming years as the federal government attempted to maintain equilibrium in the bilateral balance of trade between the island and the mainland.

In working toward legislative consensus, the domestic industry was divided between the beet sugar interests of the western states and cane growers in the south, mainly

Louisiana, at the time. The beet industry had more political clout, but could not produce enough to satisfy demand, so the two always coalesced into a single effort to protect both. The beet industry was limited because the high entry cost of land and labor in growing beets was a brake on new capacity, whereas multiple harvests from a single planting made cane a more attractive new investment. Legislators from the western states, in control of the sugar programs in Congress, understood this reality and did everything they could to maintain a truce.

There was a third factor adding pressure to the legislative process, and that was the American ownership of a part of Cuba's productive capacity. In 1913, it was estimated that 39 of 172 mills were owned by U.S. interests.[29] After the war, investment increased, but the amount is uncertain because ownership information was kept secret.

Even within the sugar processing industry, there were disagreements. Refiners were basing decisions on the price of raw sugar, whether domestically produced or imported. They pressed for differential tariffs as Cuban *centrales*, begun during the war, were rapidly expanding Cuba's ability to produce refined sugar creating the underlying fear that they could flood the market. However, they failed to convince the Congress, during hearings for the next round of tariffs, of the need for significantly higher duties on imported refined sugar possibly due to the level of American money invested in Cuba.

During the period between World War I and the early years of the Great Depression, much of the growth in sugar production came from the duty-free territories of the United States—Puerto Rico, the Philippines and Hawaii. Beet grew little despite the protectionist tariffs, Cuba was favored by U.S. money because the lower cost of operations with the *centrales* system offered a better return on investment than Florida which was still experimenting with hybrids and fertilizers and suffering from mistakes in draining the Everglades, Louisiana sugar fields were hard hit by disease, European beet sugar was coming back onto the world markets, and the price was becoming erratic

Adding to the domestic industry's difficulty was the recruitment and retention of workers. The Immigration Act of 1924 restricted European immigration and farmers turned to Mexican labor as a replacement, leading to overcrowding of quarters, unsanitary living and working conditions, and enforcement of brutal unemployment regulations. The exploitation of immigrant workers was easy because rules were rarely enforced, resulting in employment abuses that would eventually come back to haunt Florida sugarcane growers decades later.

HURRICANE FALLOUT

Prior efforts to drain the Everglades for agriculture, such as Hamilton Disston's plantation and Napoleon Broward's desire to create the grand "Empire of the Everglades," were doomed to failure for two reasons: first, the engineering was wrong because assumptions about the nature of south Florida precipitation were flawed; and second, the combination of private and state financing was subject to the ups and downs of the market and uncertain tax revenues in the State of Florida with its notorious anti-tax bias. Yet, with all the issues facing investors, sugar was always seen as a commodity with a high risk-reward ratio.

One of the risks was weather. When the two hurricanes destroyed the towns of Clewiston and Belle Glade, home to most resident sugar workers and their families, the ferocious wind and flooding from Lake Okeechobee resulted in thousands of deaths. The toll on human life was almost unimaginable, but the devastation had one beneficial effect for the future of Florida sugar growers and processors. It brought the federal government into the picture.

When President Hoover visited Florida, one of only four southern states to support his 1928 candidacy, to assess hurricane damage, he immediately understood how to prevent future loss of human life on a grand scale—build a massive dike around Lake Okeechobee. Hoover was an engineer by training and embraced the idea that federal money and expertise would assure the project's viability and success.

Governor Doyle Carlton, a big sugar booster who had accompanied Hoover on his visit, convinced the state legislature to create the Lake Okeechobee Flood Control District with broad powers to tax, issue revenue bonds and enter into agreements with the federal government to expedite construction of levees, drainage canals and pumps in south Florida. The district's jurisdiction went all the way to the Keys, making it by far the most extensive and well-financed state agency to press forward with Florida's hope to create an agricultural paradise from the muck.

The short-term effect of Hoover's visit was a Congressional appropriation of nearly $10 million to begin construction of the dike, but it was the long-term consequence that mattered much more. With federal involvement and the introduction of the U.S. Army Corps of Engineers, a final solution to the drainage issue was within reach. It allowed Florida to make the argument that investors would be protected. and that the level of risk was diminished by the presence of the Corps, an argument that would pique the interest of New York money until October 1929, when the stock market crashed throwing the country into the worst economic crisis of its history.

TAMIAMI TRAIL

Another factor complicating re-engineering of the ground water system in south Florida at the time was construction of a two-lane road across the state. Barron Gift Collier, having fallen in love with southwest Florida from his home on Useppa Island, approached the Internal Improvement Fund to acquire one million acres of land, using the Swamp and Overflowed Lands Act of 1850, in exchange for completing a highway crossing the peninsula from Fort Myers to Miami.

The road had been started in 1919 but was never completed. The state wanted it done and accepted Collier's deal. Dredging and building went on for four years and the road opened in 1928, right before the Okeechobee Hurricane, cutting off part of the Big Cypress Swamp to the south and bisecting the central Everglades. There were a few culverts placed under the road to keep water flowing south, but the oozing swamp began to dry up. And the real effects would be felt seven decades later when Florida's environmental movement and the sugar industry would fight a pitched battle over the collapse of Florida Bay.

THE GREAT DEPRESSION

The Great Depression, beginning with a stock market crash in October 1929, spread throughout the world. Sugar prices were not immune, dropping from seven cents per pound to just over a penny in 1931 in two years. America was the world's leading consumer of sugar; one-third was produced domestically and the balance imported. In response to the crisis, protectionist legislation, with quotas, import controls and tariffs, spread rapidly across a wide variety of agricultural crops.

Congressional hearings were conducted in early 1930 to frame a follow-on bill to Fordney-McCumber with the intent of protecting domestic agriculture and industries from foreign competition. It was known as the Smoot-Hawley Tariff Act. In the early stages of the deepening economic crisis, the Christmas-tree bill covered almost twenty thousand items. Sugar was in the mix because one of the two sponsors, Senator Reed Smoot from Utah, was an elder and apostle in the Mormon Church and, according to one source, "Mormon farmers in the western U.S. grew sugar beets, and church leaders owned and controlled the powerful Utah-Idaho Sugar Co. that processed and sold them. Smoot fought for high tariffs on foreign sugar, often from Cuba, to help the domestic sugar beet business thrive." [30] It was not only the beet interests behind the push for tariffs, but also Bror Dahlberg of Celotex who met with Smoot every time he was in D.C.

Smoot had a bludgeoning style while conducting hearings, badgering witnesses he disagreed with and talking over their testimony in response to his questions. He was unabashed and self-assured, having survived a series of brutal hearings on the question of whether the Senate should seat a member who espoused and practiced polygamy.

Thousands of items, nearly twenty thousand, were jammed into the bill in a classic case of logrolling—where lobbyists from every industry imaginable petitioned congressmen and senators from districts and states affected by lower prices, both real and imagined, and members agreed to reciprocal support in exchange for votes in favor of their pet projects. As the bill moved from the House to the Senate, economists became alarmed, warning that aggressive tariffs would deepen the Depression. But exuberance won the day, the bill passed and with the tariff on imported sugar which moved from 1.76¢ per pound to two cents, the price of sugar, at 3.4¢ wholesale in 1930 dropped to 3¢ in 1933, due primarily to increased domestic supply coming after the tariff was raised.

Dahlberg, despite the problems afflicting his company, was active behind the scenes in formulating terms for the expansion of Florida sugar. At the peak of his power, he had a history of effective lobbying and building connections in Washington over the years. Convinced that he could break the Democratic Party's hold on the solid south by bringing Florida into the Republican column, he succeeded in doing that in the 1928 election when Herbert Hoover knocked off Al Smith. Immediately after Hoover's election, he pressed hard for federal money to drain the Everglades, and doubling the tariff on Cuban sugar believing that Florida's harvest was the logical replacement. Dahlberg failed to get his extra tariff and his company soon went into bankruptcy, but his legacy would live on as the successor corporation, with new management, would pursue the same goals with regard to Cuban sugar with even greater zest.

The Cuban sugar industry was buffeted economically by the new two cent tariff, and experienced declining export revenues because of the recession. Because of Smoot-Hawley, raw sugar production decreased on the island by 61% between 1929 and 1933. As a result, Cuban purchases of American goods during the same period declined 83%.[31] On the other hand, the tariff was structured in a way to encourage domestic producers, particularly the Philippines, to step up production which made up for reduced Cuban imports.

Part of the problem created in Cuba stemmed from the introduction of new large-scale mills into the production stream. After enactment of Smoot-Hawley, demand in the U.S. market dropped dramatically and the mills, with reduced raw sugar output, were unable to operate efficiently. Wages for workers were severely cut; the cost of producing a pound of refined sugar in Cuba went down by half, placing even more pressure on the world price.

The U.S. Tariff Commission realized this and warned that the three-way interrelationship between U.S. tariffs, costs of production in Cuba, and the world price "has not been effective either as a price protection to domestic producers, or as an encouragement to expansion in production, but has primarily served on the one hand to destroy the Cuban industry, and on the other hand to bring about continuous and very rapid expansion in Puerto Rico and the Philippines." [32]

The Smoot-Hawley tariffs exacerbated the worldwide economic picture, sunk the U.S. economy deeper into the Great Depression, and added to the growing perception that the country was headed toward isolationism.

AGRICULTURAL ADJUSTMENT ACT OF 1933 AND THE JONES–COSTIGAN ACT OF 1934

The Great Depression was the anvil against which modern sugar policy was forged. As economic activity continued to decline despite massive government support with an intervening Congress, urged on by newly elected President Franklin Roosevelt, the omnibus Agricultural Adjustment Act of 1933 (AAA) was passed in the hope that it would stabilize crop prices through government production controls by putting in place a system of payments to compensate for the reduction in crops planted and for land allowed to lie fallow. It was a classic agricultural support program with a single purpose—to stabilize prices and farm incomes. Roosevelt's desire was to achieve "parity," levels of farm income that equaled purchasing power prior to World War I.

"Parity" was not achieved quickly. It would take until 1940, and the AAA's enduring value was modified throughout the years, but one piece of the bill survives to this day—creation of the Commodity Credit Corporation (CCC). Established to "stabilize, support and protect farm income and prices," the government-owned corporation was given the power to buy and sell land and perform other activities to accomplish its mission. Today, the CCC is the pass-through agency for payments that subsidize sugar processors.

Despite efforts by Senator Edward Costigan of Colorado, sugar was not included as a "basic commodity" in the AAA when the bill moved from the Senate where it passed, to the House where it failed. Colorado grew a small amount of beet sugar, so despite failure in the House he remained active in promoting legislation that would include sugar as a necessary commodity. He had been appointed by President Wilson to the United States Tariff Commission in 1917, serving for eleven years while practicing law, before running for the Senate in 1930. He was a reformer by nature so having fair labor standards in any legislation was an important factor to both him and his wife.

When the AAA failed to include sugar, as a compromise the industry was given an opportunity to work out a cooperative marketing plan to control production. The discussions, held among competitors, were exempted from anti-trust prosecution. But differing interests between cane and beet, and the various regions of the country and some U.S. territories, made it impossible to reach agreement. And, Cuban interests were not included in discussions leading up to the drafting of the bill, leaving out the world's major sugar producer and one of America's largest export markets for manufactured goods.

The inexorable intertwining of American and Cuban interests was again complicated by the decline of Cuban sugar being imported into the U.S. As a result, the country's financial stress led to a severely diminished ability to buy American-made products. Plus, Cuba was bordering on political instability, after suffering from falling employment and incomes, giving President Franklin Roosevelt multiple arguments that propping up the country's economy was desirable for both business and hemispheric relations.

The drop in Cuban exports to the U.S. had one bright side though—stabilization of imports from duty-free territories of the Philippines, Hawaii and Puerto Rico. Upon reviewing the reasons for failure to negotiate a cooperative agreement, and in order to boost Cuban purchase of American goods, Roosevelt then took a giant step. He asked the Congress in 1934 to stabilize the price by limiting production in the U.S. and its territories. It represented a sea change in the way prices would be controlled.

The cost of the U.S. sugar program was also weighing heavily on consumers. Protectionist legislation had taken a crop valued at $60 million in market value to a cost to consumers of over $200 million. The Roosevelt administration was convinced the sugar industry was raising the price to consumers unfairly and they were determined to keep the cost to the public down.

Costigan then took the reins from his good friend the president. He sponsored a bill to amend the AAA along with Representative Marvin Jones of Texas, chairman of the House Agriculture Committee. The amendment would include sugar as a "basic commodity," and despite pressure from the sugar refiners vigorously opposed to production quotas, the bill sought to deal with three other important parties at interest: growers, processors and farm laborers.

To compensate farmers for any losses they might suffer from government-imposed limits on production through allotments, the administration proposed a tax on processors—being the difference between the "fair exchange value" of the crop and the market price. The tax could be adjusted to ensure that inventories remained low and prices were not artificially depressed. Proceeds from the tax would be returned to farmers as a subsidy of one-half cent for every pound they produced, not as a direct payment but through the purchase of crop surplus to help feed people during the Depression. It was characterized as a "rental payment."

Beet and cane processors were each given a percentage of the overall allotments based upon the processing plant's location and the Secretary of Agriculture's estimate of total annual domestic consumption. This method continues to the present day and gives the secretary enormous power in setting parameters on production.

The bill also attempted to address the complicated issue of "parity" between incomes generated from farm operations when compared to manufactured products. Most products were made by corporations, whereas farming in the 1930s tended to be run by families. Before the Depression, led by Henry Ford's new technique of assembling the 1928 Model A, and labor saving devices such as the washing machine coming on to the market, industrial America was increasing its work force by pulling people from the fields to the cities, and the Secretary of Agriculture, Henry Wallace, was pressing Roosevelt to provide financial aid to farmers to ensure that agriculture remained viable. Wallace felt that international competitors were heavily subsidized by governments with the added advantage of cheaper labor. With collapsing prices, there was growing concern in Washington that American agriculture was failing, that farmers would simply walk away as banks foreclosed on loans, with the result that the country would not be able to feed itself across a broad array of foods.

The final piece of the legislation set forth fair labor standards laws applying to workers in the beet and cane fields. At the insistence of the senator's wife, Mabel, whose life had been devoted to promoting child labor laws, children under the age of fourteen were not permitted to work in the fields or mills; those from ages fourteen to sixteen were limited to eight-hour days. The bill also gave the Secretary of Agriculture expanded powers to intervene and settle disputes between growers, processors and their workers, a power which would be sorely tested periodically over the next sixty years.

Price stabilization would be accomplished by government allotments—as opposed to tariffs—the first-time quotas were used in an attempt to control sugar prices. The operative principle was that by limiting supply coming onto the market each year, the price could be controlled from the supply side of the equation, if the market was limited to the U.S. and possessions and insulated from competing countries like Java.

With an eye to Caribbean sugar, particularly Cuba, there was a limit set to both U.S. territories and foreign sources based upon the average tonnage produced domestically and imported between 1925 and 1933. The years chosen were 1931 – 1933 and the quotas were as follows in short tons:

Beet sugar	1,556,166
Puerto Rico	802,842
Hawaii	916,500
Philippines	1,015,186
Cuba	1,901,752
Virgin Islands	5,470
Cane sugar	261,034 [33]

The quotas showed how relatively insignificant Louisiana and Florida cane growers and processors were in the assignment of market allotments. Over time, that would change, but in 1934 the future of sugar in the State of Florida looked rather dim, until the appearance of U.S. Sugar Corporation's president, Clarence Bitting, who would take Florida's message to the Congress with astonishing results.

ENDURING TRENDS

The Jones-Costigan amendment, known also as the Sugar Act of 1934, established the conceptual and mechanism framework for the sugar industry of today. The government enshrined the mechanisms to regulate production, importation and the price of sugar. Tariffs would still be applied, but it was a number of new elements that set the stage for the growth of the domestic sugar industry, and for Florida to finally begin to realize its full potential.

In summary, at the heart of the bill were four provisions that would survive the ages. The first was creation of marketing allotments to control domestic production, and presumably prices, a major departure from the singular use of tariffs, dating back to the eighteenth century, as a means of manipulating the price of sugar in the domestic market. Control of production would take place through allotments between beet and cane. Second was authorization for the government to purchase any surplus of beet sugar. The third provision related only to the refined product giving the Secretary to duty to set allotments and quotas based upon a prediction of annual domestic demand. Finally, subsidies to growers, in the form of "rental payments" were introduced.

One controversial provision in the bill was the "rental payment," the power granted to the Secretary to set a processing tax "to prevent inventory buildup and depression of agricultural prices." [34] It was knocked out in 1936 by the U.S. Supreme Court in the *Hoosic vs Mills* case. The government had no power to absolutely restrict the acreage put into production but decided to use a system that had worked for other crops—an incentive for keeping acreage fallow. The processing tax was set at 50¢ per 100 pounds for raw sugar and higher for refined sugar, applied to both domestic and imported sources. Incentive payments to growers would be 60¢ per 100 pounds.[35] The court ruled that the processing tax was unconstitutional, but quotas could remain in place.

After the court's decision, the Roosevelt administration responded with the Soil Conservation and Domestic

Allotment Act of 1936, allowing direct payments to farmers for a number of crops with certain conditions, followed quickly by the Sugar Act of 1937, wherein funds appropriated by Congress would be used for payments in lieu of the processing tax.

SUGAR ACT OF 1937

When the Supreme Court ruled that the tax on processors used to reimburse sugar farmers for taking land out of production was unconstitutional, Congress had responded by tweaking the terms of the 1934 amendment, moving from a processor tax to an excise tax payable into the General Fund. With this additional step, Congress could then appropriate money for payment to farmers who met stipulated conditions. In all other respects, the legislation was similar, save one major difference: quotas for mainland production were increased by 50% due to new capacity— mainly benefiting Florida as a result of lobbying efforts by Clarence Bitting, president of the U.S. Sugar Corporation, accompanied by Frank Heiser of Fellsmere Sugar Producers Association.

The quota system decoupled the price of sugar in the United States from the rest of the world. The earlier tariff system established a price floor equal to the world price plus the import duty. The new system set a limit on the amount that processors could sell. It worked best when consumption, i.e. demand, was completely filled by all the pre-established quotas. The one problem with the system was that with a ceiling on the amount of sugar that could be sold by processors and refiners, it kept a lid on the amount of raw sugar, both beet and cane, that refiners could buy. But if the annual quota was not met, imports would be brought into fill the gap. With that, the price differential (with London price expressed in U.S. currency) in cents per pound of raw sugar was:

Year	London Price ¢	New York Price
1926	2.62	2.59
1927	2.91	2.96
1928	2.49	2.45
1929	1.91	2.00
1930	1.38	1.48
1931	1.25	1.34
1932	0.87	0.93
1933	0.97	1.23
1934	1.04	1.50
1935	1.00	2.33
1936	1.01	2.69
1937	1.32	2.54
1938	1.14	2.04
1939	1.60	1.91
1940	1.33	1.89
1941	1.85	2.48 [36]

The impact of the quota system is obvious as shown on the chart above. And since Cuba had a large part of the import quota, its economy received a substantial benefit from the system, helping to restore the balance of trade between the two countries. Farm incomes in the U.S. increased, and by 1940, President Roosevelt declared that "parity" had been achieved for those tillers of the soil in the American sugar industry.

Corporate Farming Begins in Florida

CLARENCE BITTING AND U.S. SUGAR CORPORATION

What was becoming increasingly significant to the future of the sugarcane business in Florida during the Great Depression were the efforts of one man, single-minded in his determination to make the state the sugar-producing center of the country. Pressing the Roosevelt administration for higher quotas, he was largely responsible for some of the terms of the Sugar Act of 1937. That man was Clarence Bitting, president of the United States Sugar Corporation (USSC).

Charles Stewart Mott, a vice president of General Motors and entrepreneur, had merged his company, Weston-Mott, which made wheels for automobiles into General Motors. He had a seat on the board and a chunk of stock. In 1929, he and members of his family along with other associates purchased a controlling interest—68%—in the bankrupt Southern Sugar Company.

Clarence Bitting, in on the deal, was named president. He was a technocrat, well-groomed and educated as an accountant at the University of Pennsylvania, heading his own consulting company and a friend of Fred Fisher, who owned Fisher Body Corporation before it became part of General Motors. He and his brother owned 10% of USSC stock, so he had a strong vested interest in the company's future.

Bitting was a good manager and a superbly effective corporate propagandist. He orchestrated a public relations blitz publishing numerous articles on management of large enterprises, placing himself before multiple Congressional committees. In today's parlance, he would be a registered lobbyist. He even chartered a train in 1936 to bring one hundred legislators from Washington on a junket to see the company's sugar fields in Florida and play a little golf on the side.

Those operations were infused with corporate paternalism. Bitting and Mott both believed that workers, whether seasonally migrant or residential, should be well cared for. But before implementing measures to create better working conditions, Bitting had to put USSC on a profitable footing.

He did so using two standard industrial techniques: scientific research for product improvement and strict cost controls. The science produced a new variety of sugarcane, known as the F31-962 which was both disease and frost resistant. It was planted in over half the company's fields by 1938.[37] The company's mill, processing 7,000 tons per day, was a model of efficiency designed and sized to take advantage of economies of scale.

The Sugar Act of 1937 also offered Bitting the opportunity to engage smaller growers in a joint venture that would feed harvested cane into the company's large mill. The group, known as the Florida Cooperative Sugar Association, adopted the Cuban *centrales* model for the domestic product but also served another useful purpose. It would blunt mounting criticism that USSC was a brutal monopolist trying to run its competitors out of business.

But there was a large grain of truth to that claim. Bitting was, in fact, doing his level best to run both Louisiana and Cuban cane growers and processors out of business. He saw the sugar business as a "zero-sum game" in which quotas taken from one would be given to another. The eight growers in the cooperative were mainly speculators who had bought cane-growing land from smaller, bankrupt farmers. They were the backdrop of a strategy to make the struggle for increased quotas appear to be a fight by the small Florida farmers for a piece of the pie. Louisiana, on the other hand, was the real deal with over twelve thousand small farmers involved in growing sugarcane, and a carefully orchestrated public relations campaign.

Despite the obvious disparity, Bitting had an important politician up his sleeve, and that was Senator Claude Pepper (D-FL), always eager to please a well-heeled constituent.

Bitting, with the cooperative behind him to help finance campaigns, enlisted the senator to increase quotas every year. Pepper had the ear of President Roosevelt and had been instrumental in formulating the White House message to Congress in pressing for the 1934 Act, so was intimately familiar with the issues confronting his well-heeled constituents.

The result of Bitting and Pepper's effectiveness is shown in the chart below showing final adjusted quotas in short tons (rounded):

	1934	1940
U.S. beet sugar	1,556,000	1,550,000
U.S. cane sugar	261,000	420,000
Hawaii	917,000	938,000
Puerto Rico	803,000	798,000
Philippines	1,015,000	982,000
Cuba	1,902,000	1,749,000 [38]

The reduction in Cuba's quota was part of a long-term strategy to move as much cane production to Florida as possible, creating better economies of scale for USSC operations.

Once the company was solid financially ($1 million in profit in 1938), Bitting turned to creating an efficient workplace, but what was curious was his lack of interest in mechanization for the harvest, the *zafra*. Having put so much money behind scientific research and processing efficiency, it would have been a normal course to either renew the Pennsuco experiments or attempt to adapt the Falkiner harvesting machines developed in Australia in 1925 to Florida's soils.

The Falkiner harvester had fascinated Bror Dahlberg. He bought the patent rights from its Australian founder and had fourteen of the machines built. The Falkiner had rotating cutters at ground level and a blower fan that would elevate the overhanging leaves at the top of the plant. But it got bogged down too easily in Everglades muck and slicing at the base was uneven. With a shallow root system, the plant could be torn from the ground.

Instead of working on mechanization, the company and Bitting turned to the methods of Frederic Winslow Taylor, the industrial engineer who created the modern automobile assembly line at Ford Motor Company. Taylor, a Philadelphian like Bitting, believed that the careful analysis of workflow could translate into the reduction or elimination of unnecessary steps in the process and workers could be convinced to both understand and appreciate efforts to make their output more productive.

Bitting sat astride two views of the Jim Crow south in the 1930s and 1940s. The first was neo-plantationism and the other was creation of a social benefit from corporate welfare.[39] Whether Bitting's treatment of workers was sincere or simply a reaction to the Roosevelt administration's liberal bent is open to question. What Bitting probably sensed was that an enlightened paternalistic approach to workers, paying them a fair wage, housing them and educating their families, could form a barrier to unionization.

How workers were treated in other countries was always part of USSC's argument to increase quotas for Florida. Seeking the high ground, Bitting's pamphlets explored, in the minutest terms, conditions in Cuba described as oppressive and exploitive. But Bitting didn't stop there. His scorched earth policy expanded to attack territorial sugarcane growers including Hawaii, the Philippines and Puerto Rico. Florida's newspapers joined in with pungent editorials and devastating cartoons boosting the opportunity to create American jobs as the sugar industry grew.

But there was a dark side to the boosterism. Photographs of USSC's worker villages taken at the time by inquiring journalists, but never printed in the company's brochures, put one in mind of the long, dirt streets in South Carolina's rice plantations and Alabama's cotton fiefdoms.

1937 INTERNATIONAL SUGAR AGREEMENT

The Cuban government, always concerned about price fluctuations and rapidly changing conditions, was looking for ways to influence the international sugar market. It had asked the League of Nations to look into the matter in 1927, after the country's quota to the U.S., just shy of 4 million tons in 1926, dropped to 3.5 million tons in 1927 and prospects were for further decreases. The main problem was Java. Controlled by the Netherlands, sugar production was thriving and the Dutch colony had succeeded in cross-fertilizing two cane varieties to produce a higher per plant yield.

With higher productivity and lower costs, the Dutch were simply not interested in participating in any agreement that would control supply on the world market. Little was done until 1929 when a group meeting in Geneva, without the United States, began to work on a cooperative arrangement among participating producers. The European beet processors were having difficulty holding their export markets, and Java cane sugar was flooding the Far East, so agreement was desirable but elusive.

In order to bring some sense to the wildly fluctuating market, Cuba then subscribed to the Chadbourne Plan, an attempt to stabilize the price by restricting supply through creation of massive stockpiles of sugar. It was the brainchild of Thomas Chad-Bourne, a New York lawyer, with a number of clients having large investments in Cuba.

The deal, known as the International Sugar Agreement, was signed in 1931 by a number of European nations and Java, and began to stabilize the market. But the following year, as the plan sought to impose stricter controls on production and marketing, the worldwide Depression overwhelmed potential restrictions as U.S. banks, owners of much of Cuba's stockpiled sugar surplus, began to sell inventory to maintain solvency, driving the price of sugar down again.

The plan ended up hurting native Cuban growers, fueling anti-American sentiment harkening back to memories of the Platt Amendment of 1902 which allowed the U.S. to intervene militarily to preserve life and property—particularly property owned by American interests. Cubans, who had bought into the Chadbourne Plan in the beginning, felt the U.S. was ignoring their desire to be a sovereign nation after throwing off the chains of Spanish ownership and control, and concluded that the plan was simply another subterfuge toward greater foreign control of the island.

By 1933, with slowing economic activity worldwide and with the United States quota now at 1.6 million tons, Cuba proposed a series of steps to stabilize the amount of sugar being dumped on the world market, but the concept of restraint was vetoed by a small number of powerful countries including Great Britain. But by 1937, having stabilized their own markets, both Britain and the United States pressed for control of exports. Quotas were agreed to by the twenty-two signatories including the world's largest exporter at the time, the Netherlands and all its possessions, mainly Java. An international commission was formed to oversee the agreement, and the U.S. agreed to (1) maintain levels of imports paying the full protective tariff that had been enacted with the Sugar Act of 1937 and (2) allow any additional supply to come from imports if domestic growers failed to meet the quotas of processors.

Despite its participation, the United States pressed

forward in legislation with its desire to go its own way when it came to pricing. The 1937 International Sugar Agreement was directed mainly at ensuring an adequate supply to consumers at a fair price, but no enforceable pricing mechanism was included. The agreement was delayed by slow ratification and effective for only two years, falling apart as countries anticipating the beginning of World War II, in September 1939, began to stockpile supplies by purchasing from countries that had not signed on. Once war began, the only survivor of the agreement was the International Sugar Council, with the thought that once the war was over there should be a mechanism in place to pull the pieces back together.

A CLOSER LOOK AT THE U.S. SUGAR BUSINESS IN 1941

The main elements of the 1934 and 1937 acts were implementation of a quota system for production and marketing of sugar as a means of controlling price. The U.S. had experience with government-mandated quotas and a robust agricultural reporting system in place, making the transition to wartime regulations easier. European countries, having subsidized sugar for years, had built substantial stockpiles in anticipation of war on the continent. The U.S. had also built up significant inventory, 1.6 million short tons by September 1939, thanks to a robust harvest.[40] But by 1941 the international situation was beginning to produce havoc in the world market.

A Senate Finance Committee hearing held in March 1941 revealed the structure of the sugar industry in the United States just before the war. There were no Florida senators on the committee, but among the twenty-five witnesses, Senator Charles Andrews from Florida spoke before the assemblage.[41]

His testimony was a paean to his home state, and a masterful argument obscuring reality. He opened by admitting that Florida produced only 1% of the sugar consumed in America. He then continued:

"There are some other matters in connection with our present allotment policy that I will not mention at this time, other than to say that down in Florida there was paid nearly $500,000 for the nonuse of lands lying idle, the richest of which exceeds the Valley of the Nile. Cane matures 8 and 10 feet high there in that rich soil, and the Government pays them not to use it. I introduced an amendment in the Senate past year offering to forfeit this if they will let us plant our acreage without restriction, and thus build up at home a great industry for our own American farmers." [42]

Andrews went on to describe his constituents:

"In that cane-producing area there are 5,000 or 6,000 men, most of them heads of families, who are making a living by raising sugarcane. Whether they own the land themselves or not, they have to be farmers to cultivate sugarcane, and the farm laborers are paid $2 a day and spend every penny of it in the United States. They buy automobiles from Michigan, and they buy various manufacturing goods from other parts of the United States with that money. The economic situation is such that in some of the areas where we are importing sugar, labor is paid less than one-third of that paid in Florida; and even that money never gets back here." [43]

What is remarkable is the obfuscation about the Florida farmer. The reality, of course, was that sugar was being grown and processed at the time by one very large corporation and that "making a living by raising sugarcane" did not necessarily mean that the heads of families were farming their own land.

In contrast, C. J. Bourg spoke on behalf of the 9,671 sugarcane growers in Louisiana, all members of the American Sugar Cane League. A number of jobs were at stake and the issue at hand was the possible quota deficit from the Philippines. The shortfall, under terms of the Sugar Act of 1937, would be allocated among other foreign producers.

During the hearing, Senator Alva Adams from Colorado, one of the bill's sponsors, stated that:

"... (t)he sugar-beet industry is a small-farm operation. In my state the beet acreage is 10, 20 and 30 acres. .... It is a unit type production. That is, you have your sugar factory and your sugar-beet production, and they make up a unit. If the factory closes, sugar beets cannot be produced." [44]

Alva went on to say that it took about 10,000 acres of farmed beets to sustain a mill producing raw sugar. The state at the time had seventeen factories but an allocation of only 136,000 acres, which meant that four factories would have to close unless the quota for Colorado was raised. He went on to argue that by allowing deficits to be made up by domestic producers rather than imports, American jobs would be saved.

What is most interesting about the hearing is how different the situation was when comparing the number of farmers in beet growing states, and Louisiana sugarcane grower's association with over nine thousand members, to Florida at the time. U.S. Sugar dominated the business in Florida and, despite its lower quota, was operating as a fully integrated business rather than using a working arrangement such as the one between producers and refiners in the beet growing states. But Florida was only a single state with little political power as compared to beet sugar being grown in ten states at the time.

Later, in 1941 after Pearl Harbor, the House of Representatives voted on a bill to prop up import quotas from Cuba given the need for raw sugar in munitions. At the hearing, Senator Claude Pepper, assiduously courted by Clarence Bitting of U.S. Sugar, described the situation:

"Now, I said at one time here in this committee that I did not favor monopoly in my State any more than I favored it in any other State in the Union. Now, this one corporation started in the production of sugarcane in Florida. I attended the first opening of its mill in 1929. It got under way. It was able to experiment on a large scale and it had capital which was largely supplied by industrialists. One of the big corporations, the General Motors Corporation, is one of the principal stockholders in this company. Very few of them are Florida people. They have come in and established a great business and I am proud of them, we want to encourage it but the way this sugar bill operates in Florida, they are in fact granted a relative monopoly in the production and refinement of sugarcane in our State." [45]

Pepper went on to admit that U.S. Sugar had 85% of the market in Florida and either owned or controlled 20,000 of the 24,000 acres allotted to growing cane plants. 3,000 of the remaining acres were farmed by Fellsmere Farms and the last 1,000 by small farmers.

It was tacitly understood that the appearance of cooperation between beet and cane growers was essential in Washington politics, but the sugar business itself continued to be fraught with internal problems. The issue of the moment was the refining industry, opposed to the amendment. Ellsworth Bunker, who would later become ambassador to four different countries and one of the leading hawks on the Vietnam War, appeared representing the United States Cane Sugar Refiners Association. He was joined by refiners from Baltimore (and the city's mayor), an organization titled Committee for the Defense of Philadelphia Sugar Refining Industry and by two local union presidents from Philadelphia, all in opposition to Adams' bill.

Here again was a stark contrast to the situation in Florida, where unions were non-existent and vertical integration from farm to refined product was the operative business model. Even in 1941, cane syrup produced in Florida would be refined in Florida as a harbinger of changes in the industry yet to come.

SUGAR IN WORLD WAR II

When war broke out in Europe prices increased rapidly but settled back down after the initial shock of Hitler's panzers wore off. By the attack on Pearl Harbor in 1941, total inventory and production had declined mainly because of beet sugar dropping from 1.6 million tons in 1941 to 1 million tons in 1943 due to the loss of field workers leaving for higher-paying factory jobs in the defense industries. On the other hand, sugarcane in the U.S. increased during the same period, but not enough to make up the loss from beet processors. Part of the reason was that the cane-growing soils along the Gulf Coast were not easily converted to growing other crops as was the case with beet farms.

To balance supply for both consumers and war needs, the Department of Agriculture set goals for almost all crops beginning in 1943. The goals had little to do with price and a great deal to do with the need to maintain an adequate supply, but as the war dragged on both beet and cane were slowly decreased to keep prices stable and maintain farm incomes at reasonable levels. The department had capped the price in 1941. As the price rose, additional marketing allowances were granted, but failed to slow the increases. The government then shifted gears and decided to put on a price cap at 3.5¢ per pound. The ceiling increased until 1946 when it reached 4.205¢.[46]

The other way of maintaining an adequate supply throughout the system was to control demand by rationing. Varying from six to twenty pounds per person in a household, a ration book was issued with stamps for a base amount and then local boards were able to adjust supplies from applications based upon need.

Finally, to ensure that the country would have enough sugar, the Commodity Credit Corporation purchased all raw sugar imported from Puerto Rico and Cuba and then resold it to domestic refiners. In the case of Cuba, its entire crop was purchased beginning in 1943. Hawaiian sugar was shipped directly to the West Coast under the aegis of the

War Shipping Board; reporting was consistent throughout the agencies responsible for balancing supply, demand and price. The system, while fraught with occasional missteps, worked fairly well during the course of the war.

Cuba was an essential partner to the United States at this time. The two governments worked out a series of agreements that would give the U.S. defense industry as much of Cuba's production as it could spare. The main reason for government emphasis was that sugar was central to the war effort. Industrial alcohol and acetone, from blackstrap and invert molasses, had been used in the manufacture of munitions during World War I, and became even more necessary in the second war as natural rubber from Malaysia was interdicted by the Japanese and synthetic rubber took its place. As the raw material for making acetone, blackstrap molasses is available during the later stages of beet and cane sugar processing. Invert molasses from sugarcane comes earlier in the process and is cheaper than other grains like corn in making alcohol. And while chemically different, acetone and alcohol are used for many of the same purposes such as fuel additives.

Cuba sold an average of 900,000 equivalent tons of raw sugar and large quantities of 190 proof industrial alcohols in the three years from 1943 to 1946. By distilling the alcohol at home, Cuba could keep its plants running at near capacity and the country fully employed. The agreed to price was $2.65 per hundred pounds until 1945 when it went to $3.10. The following year $3.675 was scheduled unless certain escalator conditions were met, which would boost the price to $4.816.[47]

With its importance demonstrated by the rapid rise in the negotiated price, sugar was a strategic commodity in the early days of the war. It was the first crop to be rationed in the United States, and last to be taken off the ration list. It was the subject of a major public relations effort to describe its importance in the war effort from munitions to emergency rations carried by airmen as survival food. There is another school of thought that the underlying reason for emphasizing sugar to the American public, given their taste for sweets, was a disguised attempt to convey a message of the importance of participating in rationing to support a war that did not touch their country's shores.

The government, in addition to price controls and quotas, continued "conditional" payments to processors. The practice, begun in 1934 with the Jones-Costigan Amendment, continued during the war at 60¢ per 100 pounds through 1941. It was raised to 80¢ in 1942, a year when the Commodity Credit Corporation began another series of payments, one for excess costs created by the hardships of the war and another for inducement to increase production.

The excess cost reimbursement was for added costs of storing and transporting raw sugar from other countries, including Cuba. Freight rates had increased and the constant threat of German submarines in the Caribbean played havoc with shipping routes. In addition, processed sugar had to be moved around the country to refineries that were underutilized and in the case of beets where plants had been closed due to a lack of sugar beet production due to a shortage of labor. Finally, as the price of refined sugar was carefully managed, corn syrup and molasses were not. So, many Florida growers and processing mill owners chose to not grind out raw sugar but to keep as much as possible in molasses and syrup which could be sold at a higher price. Sugar beets, in processing, do not produce an edible variety of molasses, so processors were stuck with the refined product while their competitors in Louisiana and Florida were free to do as they wished.

Finally, the war was a boon to Florida's sugarcane industry. With rationing and limited supplies, coupled with the strategic importance of the crop, the argument was effectively made that Florida had enormous unused capacity if the Everglades could be drained. It also had arable land being used for other purposes, mainly cattle and lemon grass, and could be quickly converted to growing cane plants.

Clarence Bitting and Senator Claude Pepper pointed this out in multiple Congressional hearings. In addition the U.S. Sugar Corporation, backed by heavy government-funded research into soils and hybrid plants, had managed to get the yield up to thirty tons per acre, nearly double that of Louisiana.[48] Using mechanization and vertical integration of operations from the cane field to rail transport to two massive mills, the company had available over 150,000 acres ready to plant. The war set the table for Florida's further growth as the nation's premiere sugar producer, but, as always, there was the stumbling block ninety miles south—Cuba.

Sugar After World War II

This period is of particular interest because in it were the sparks that eventually flamed into the Cuban Revolution and overthrow of the Batista government with the result that Florida's sugar barons were handed the opportunity to expand their operations exponentially. In retrospect, it may have been the flint of the United States Congress that struck those sparks.

SUGAR ACT OF 1948

Once the Axis powers were defeated, the U.S. was flooded with sugar and all rationing and controls were lifted. Quota provisions put in place in 1942 had been temporarily lifted and were due to expire in 1947. The domestic industry, both beet and cane, saw an opening to have allotments revised in their favor, but the government felt an obligation to Cuba as a result of the country's high level of bilateral cooperation in the war effort. The outcome was the Sugar Act of 1948.

Rather than an amendment to an existing bill, the new act was an attempt to make a clean break with the past. In reality, it was a restatement of the main provisions of the 1934 and 1937 legislation, but with greater specificity. The Secretary of Agriculture was still charged with calculating the domestic sugar requirement for the coming year, but the methodology was set forth with greater clarity requiring a detailed analysis of the relationship between the wholesale price of refined sugar and the cost of living (as calculated by the Consumer Price Index) in the U.S. to set quotas that would stabilize the price to consumers, producers and processors. Since the connection between price and estimated consumption was tenuous at best, other factors always worked into the final determination.

A second mandated change was that quotas would be set in short tons allocated among processors, not percentages of total estimated consumption. In 1948, this would amount to a little over 4.2 million tons. Any deficit would be offered at 95% to Cuba and 5% to other countries. The 1937 act had the deficit spread throughout the world, so the change was welcomed by Cuban companies. From 1948 to 1952, this amounted to over 2 million tons at the prevailing market rate, but despite this seeming act of largesse, Cubans still remained sullen over the failed negotiations to set a firm price for the 1947 and 1948 crops.

Reading the 1948 Act from initial draft to final version,

it is clear that industry lobbyists played a large role in writing the bill. The USDA's initial draft was not satisfactory to the mainland beet and sugar interests. Agriculture Secretary Clinton Anderson came from New Mexico, a beet growing state. He was close to the farm interests, serving as a Congressman before joining Truman's cabinet and as a Senator after he left the administration. While Secretary, he was determined to ensure that processors paid a fair price to farmers, that workers received a living wage and that fair labor standards were met by adding an 80¢ per one-hundred-pound incentive to farmers meeting specific goals.

The 1948 Act was set to expire in 1957 and would serve as the basis for sugar policy until 1956. It would be amended a number of times but retained its place as the most important legislation to date, as it formed the underlying structural framework for all future modifications to the sugar price support program for the next two and a half decades.

THE HEALTH DEBATE BEGINS

The sugar industry became concerned during the war, with rationing causing decreased consumption, that the American people might adjust to lower levels of sugar in their diet. Never failing to take advantage of a good crisis, in 1943, the industry formed the Sugar Research Foundation, little more than a propaganda machine to churn out multiple papers countering the increasing number of studies showing that sugar was major contributor to human health issues like diabetes and dental caries.

The foundation, known later as the Sugar Association, with its 142,000 members, states that it was:

"The scientific voice of the U.S. sugar industry, making a difference by continuously supporting scientific research and sharing our knowledge of sugar to increase consumer understanding and confidence in the role that sugar plays in a nutritious, balanced and enjoyable diet." [49]

In retrospect, forming the foundation was brilliant because nutritionists, medical researchers and government health experts were convinced that reduced sugar in the diet would improve public health, but there were few public voices on the other side of the debate. Research into the health effects of sugar was always part of the background noise but would take on added importance and momentum in the 1970s when high fructose corn syrup came on the market, and the American population's waistline began to slowly expand.

Farm Workers in the Sugar Fields

Another critical point of emphasis for sugar growers and processors was on bringing field hands, many of whom had migrated to larger cities and were leaving the military, back into the work force. Despite attempts to mechanize during the war, workers were needed in the fields and finding them would not be easy.

Conditions after World War II magnified one of the major problems confronting the Florida sugar business: how to recruit, train and manage people willing to work long hours in hot fields filled with pests. During the years while slavery was practiced in the South, there was seemingly no problem with finding enough black workers for the fields. Men were forced to work interminable hours under frightful conditions and women and children on sugar plantations were used for jobs in the processing plants, requiring less physical labor but equally demanding under harsh and unsavory circumstances.

Once Emancipation became the law of the land, workers had to be paid a small wage to entice them into the fields. The African-American population of the south during Reconstruction was hard put to find work, sometimes sharecropping, but a large number emigrated from Louisiana up the Mississippi to northern cities where they believed there were more jobs, diminishing the availability of field workers in the south. To satisfy the need for workers, illegal immigration increased from South American and Caribbean countries in pursuit of higher pay in the U.S.

World War I brought about labor shortages and the government, responding to pressure from southwestern states, passed a guest worker law permitting illiterates from Mexico over the age of sixteen to enter the country. The *bracero* program was expanded to include some menial non-farm jobs but was discontinued in 1922 with pressure from the AFL-CIO arguing there was no longer a national emergency and American workers were being replaced by immigrants.

Guest worker programs were originally designed to cope with labor shortages during times of national emergency and were always intended to be temporary as was the case with the *braceros*. However, the advantages of having low wage workers, easily satisfied with minimal accommodations and services, were favored by employers in agriculture. The argument was that the American worker, accustomed to good wages and a higher standard of living, had little interest in doing menial jobs—an argument that possessed more than just a glimmer of truth. According to one report, in 1932 USSC advertised for 100 jobs in the Fort Lauderdale newspaper. Only two people applied.

The need for workers in Florida expanded dramatically during the 1930s. In the 1920s, the state's quota amounted to less than 5% of domestic sugar production, but due to the efforts of Clarence Bitting and Senator Spessard Holland (D-FL), the state began to increase its capacity, quota and harvest at a rate that placed strain on growers to find enough workers, a situation that was manageable during the job-deprived Depression years. Growers and processors went to great lengths to hire reliable workers, and in 1934, the Fellsmere Sugar Company had built a small migrant village to house and service 400 workers from the British West Indies as means of attracting islanders. But domestic workers, mainly African Americans at the time, knew that cutting cane was grueling and brutal in the Florida sun. If they could first find work in the fruit and vegetable farms, that's where they went.

BWI PROGRAM

Farming sugarcane involves three basic functions: planting, weeding and harvesting. The most intensive need for labor is during the harvest season. As the Second World War began to recruit men into military service, and others into the wartime industries of the North and Midwest, California beet growers realized that the harvest was in jeopardy and convinced President Roosevelt to have the State Department negotiate a deal with Mexico to allow migrants to take temporary agricultural jobs in the U.S. Crossing the border was common at the time, and had been for years, despite loose restrictions that had been quickly reversed for mass deportations during the Depression when it was widely assumed that Mexicans were willing to work for a lower wage and take jobs away from U.S. citizens, a refrain to be repeated over and over to the present day.

The U.S. Sugar Corporation had been recruiting most of its workers from adjacent states, running trains into Clewiston filled with migrants. The company, after being purchased by Mott, built housing and schools to accommodate full-time workers for planting and weeding and managing other parts of field operations before and after the harvest. Migrants were regarded as a lower class of worker who became cane cutters because they had neither the desire nor ability to manage their own affairs as sharecroppers. And since U.S. Sugar was the dominant force in Florida at the time, its practices and philosophy regarding workers was characteristic of the prevailing norms.

USSC's dictum of stringent cost control meant that the company would resist paying higher wages to attract workers for harvest and, with its outsized political clout in Washington, convinced the government through the Farm Security Administration (FSA), part of the U.S. Department of Agriculture (USDA), to negotiate an agreement with the

Bahamas and Jamaica in 1943 to recruit workers to come into the U.S. and work in the fields. Known as the British West Indies (BWI) program (because it included Barbados, St. Vincent, St. Lucia and Dominica as well as the Bahamas) it was small when compared to the *bracero* program, allowing about 19,000 nonimmigrant workers a year to enter and leave the country between 1943 and 1947.[50] Most of them ended up in Florida, and since they spoke English were preferred by the sugar industry.

The bill, Public Law 45, was basically written by lobbyists from the American Farm Bureau. It lacked provisions guaranteeing adequate housing and a minimum wage and took the FSA out of the picture by ceding control of the program to local authorities once the workers had been recruited by the FSA. Despite its obvious flaws, the agreement was helpful to Caribbean governments and colonial administrators. The Depression had created unrest and the war had caused the tourist business to dry up. Unemployment was high among young men throughout the island populations, and the fear of revolution was always in the air.

As the program opened the borders to nonimmigrant workers, they were distributed among ten states in the northeast. But the governing statute contained a provision that workers could not leave the county in which they were scheduled to work without the permission of the local agricultural agent, a practice which amounted to indentured servitude. According to one source, a letter was written to the Department of Agriculture stating that "...(t)he vast difference between the Bahama Island labor and domestic, including Puerto Rican, is that labor transported from the Bahama Islands can be deported and sent home, if it does not work, which cannot be done in the instance of labor from domestic United States or Puerto Rico." [51]

The role of the FSA was coordinated with the U.S. Employment Service (USES), Florida State Employment Service (FSES), state Extension Service, and Sugar Section of the USDA to find workers for the sugar plantations of south Florida. The citrus and cane growers needed as much manpower as possible during picking and cutting months, with the result that the first tranche of workers from the Bahamas were brought in through Miami to pick oranges and cut cane, then immediately returned to their homeland with all transportation costs paid by the government, and not by employers.

Of all the agencies involved, the USES was most critical in filling the orchards and cane fields with workers during harvest. Farm workers under the BWI program were actually employed by the government. They signed individual contracts that set forth certain rights, a minimum wage and a set of standards covering housing food and medical care. While it looked good on paper, enforcement was lax.

The head of USES operations in Florida during and after the war was a man named Allison French. USSC had become the subject of an FBI investigation in the early

1940s for questionable labor practices and mistreatment of workers. Dozens of hearings produced characterizations by witnesses of incidents of intimidation and violence. Workers were not allowed to leave Florida plantations and forcibly returned if they tried to escape. Living conditions were abominable, with workers stacked like cordwood in railroad boxcars.

The attitude toward blacks was apparent in a number of memos circulated within government agencies but one in particular described the situation in stark and racist tones:

"When asked in local sources of labor supply had been tapped to meet the country's needs, he [French] explained that no attempt had been made to recruit Florida labor for cane cutting, first, because no definite orders were on hand and second because *Negro labor in Florida will not work for the Sugar Corporation.* Mr. French could not explain this situation except that certain "rumors" about poor treatment at the hands of Sugar Corporation foremen had always circulated among the Negro population." [52]

The report continued that workers were beaten after failing to pay company commissary debts and others had been forced to work eighteen-hour days cutting cane. To declare this sort of evidence as "rumors" speaks to the deliberate disregard of French and others as to treatment of workers.

According to the *New York Times:*

"In 1942, the Department of Justice began a major investigation into the recruiting practices of one of the largest sugar producers in the nation, the United States Sugar Corporation, a South Florida company. Black men unfamiliar with the brutal nature of the work were promised seasonal sugar jobs at high wages, only to be forced into debt peonage, immediately accruing the cost of their transportation, lodging and equipment—all for $1.80 a day. One man testified that the conditions were so bad, 'It wasn't no freedom; it was worse than the pen.' Federal investigators agreed. When workers tried to escape, the F.B.I. found, they were captured on the highway or 'shot at while trying to hitch rides on the sugar trains.'" [53]

The Justice Department presented its case on worker abuses to a grand jury in Tampa in 1943, but the indictment was dismissed on procedural grounds and the matter received little attention after that because the FBI was concerned with other issues related to the war.

The need for farm workers continued after the war, but most Americans had expanded employment opportunities because the economy was booming and there was little desire on the part of the American worker to return to the fields to pick vegetables and cut cane. Farmers knew this and convinced the government to renegotiate the *bracero* program to guarantee the availability of Mexican workers for harvest in the western states. The BWI program was allowed to expire in 1947 and was converted into a series of temporary worker agreements with contracts negotiated between U.S. companies, governments of the Indies involved and the workers. And despite the role of government agencies in recruiting, they were not party to the contracts. The method was unwieldy at best and led to a series of complaints from farmers as to the difficulties in recruiting workers and complaints from workers about brutal working conditions, questionable pay practices and unsanitary living quarters.

Looking back on the BWI program, growers had a good thing going. And they knew it. The wages paid to BWI cane cutters were low enough to set a ceiling on what the companies would pay domestic workers, discouraging most citizens from even applying for the job. Fair labor standards did not apply. Cutting was seasonal and it was easy to return men to the islands for a short period before coming back. The other lesson learned was that the whole scheme rested upon political muscle in Washington, a lesson that still applies in spades to today's world.

H-2 PROGRAM

To clean up the messy situation created after expiration of the BWI program, President Truman appointed a commission to study a way to hire temporary workers for various industries. Based upon the commission's recommendations, the Congress passed the Immigration and Nationality Act of 1952 authorizing a new classification of unskilled, migrant labor in what was called the H-2 program, still in effect today. The bill permitted farmers to hire provided they could prove that the same jobs had been made available to domestic workers. However, the seasonal nature of picking apples or cutting cane made the jobs unattractive for American citizens looking for steady income with the result that the H-2 program quickly became a marked success.

In addition, the relationship was governed by the terms of a written agreement, giving employers wide latitude with respect to what they would, and would not, offer in the way of services to the workers and their families. This was a sticking point with the previous BWI and *bracero* programs because many of the promises made, some in writing, were either never fulfilled or hedged.

The Florida sugar industry had lost a great deal of credibility harking back to the Jim Crow days as well as the nature of the work. The only answer lay in increased mechanization, workable for tilling and furrowing, but less so for planting and harvesting. The industry would head in that direction as events in Cuba presented a golden opportunity that would forever alter the future of growing sugar in Florida.

Sugar Politics and the Cold War

The cold war, a standoff between Russia and the allied powers of Western Europe and the United States, began right after the Yalta conference of 1945 when Churchill, Roosevelt and Stalin attempted to reach agreement as to how to partition occupied territories in Eastern and Western Europe. Beyond geography, it was also a battle between democratic capitalism and state-run socialism. The conflict was mainly political but had serious military moments—one of which was the possible placement of Russian missiles in Cuba in 1962.

The Cuban missile crisis is important because it gave the sugar industry of Florida an immediate opening to fill the domestic market with its product by expanding land under cultivation exponentially.

CUBAN REVOLUTION

Cuba had always been an edgy country and American

investors constantly sought protection of their assets harkening back to the Platt Amendment of 1902 which gave the U.S. the self-imposed right to assert military control over Cuba—a concept that remained as a constant reminder that the island was not truly independent and capable of self-determination but dominated by its imperialist neighbor ninety miles to the north.

During World War II, Fulgencio Batista was the elected president of Cuba. A military officer, he rose to power in the 1930s when the army revolted against the Céspedes government and he served as the elected head of state from 1940 to 1944, after overseeing modest reform of the country's public works and educational system. He retired to Florida as a wealthy man after his first term. He returned to his native country in 1952 to be elected president with the support of the U.S. government, but rapidly assumed a dictatorial role by controlling the military and making himself the only candidate in the 1954 and 1958 elections. His oppressive rule grated upon the peasants, particularly those in the eastern provinces that led to the rise of Fidel Castro.

Batista's social and educational programs during the war were a direct result of the relationship between his country's sugar exports and America's need for ethanol for military purposes. Cuba had always been the shock absorber for the American sugar program. Price stability could be achieved simply by altering the Cuban quota and filling in any deficits from territorial suppliers like the

Philippines and Puerto Rico.

The U.S. purchased the entire Cuban sugar crop from 1942 to 1946 at a fixed price well below the international open market price. With the Philippines out of production due to the Japanese control of the territory, the Cuban marketing tonnage numbers were:

1939	1,930,000
1940	1,750,000
1941	2,700,000
1942	1,796,000
1943	2,857,000
1944	3,618,000
1945	2,803,000
1946	2,283,000
1947	3,943,000 [54]

The Sugar Act of 1948 began to upend the Cuban boom. The island's economy during the war had become heavily dependent upon sugar with mills running full bore. It pleaded with the U.S. to maintain the highest possible level of imports. Maintaining fixed quotas, Cuba was granted 28% of the domestic market's predicted consumption and 95% of the Philippines' deficit as a temporary reward for its cooperation during the war. But one sticking point was that as the Philippines came back into full production, Cuba would lose market share.

While the main purpose of the 1948 Act was to

provide domestic industries stability and opportunities for growth, the National Resources Security Council, formed under President Truman in 1947, issued a report strongly urging that the U.S. treat its hemispheric partners carefully, as Russian hegemony was spreading throughout Southeast Asia and in Europe as far west as Greece and Turkey. The report concluded that sugar was the key to a healthy ongoing relationship with Cuba.

The Korean War interdicted the debate to give Congress a breather, but in 1952, the Cuban harvest exceeded seven million tons and all the U.S. territories were operating at full capacity. With a world surplus building rapidly so did pressure to increase domestic quotas, mainly at the expense of Cuba. Secretary of State John Foster Dulles framed the strategic situation as a clear choice: favoring American producers at the expense of a traditional trading partner vs. the possibility of political instability ninety miles to the south of Key Largo.

The sugar barons, on the other hand, saw Cuba as a competitor and not as an ally, arguing that national security interests should be placed above all else. In simple terms, this meant the more domestic production authorized, the less America would have to rely upon other countries for its supply of sugar.

1956 ACT

It all came to a head in the Sugar Bill of 1956. The industry, plagued by low prices and a massive surplus, got fourteen separate bills introduced in the House.[55] Senator Holland, whose campaign coffers had been well supplied by sugar money from Clarence Bitting and others, approached President Eisenhower in December 1955 about rewriting the 1948 act as amended before it expired. Eisenhower refused. U.S. Ambassador Arthur Gardner, a close friend of the president and a supporter of Batista, had warned that further cutbacks of Cuba's quota which at the time was 33% of domestic consumption, would result in the immediate collapse of the government. And surprisingly, Senator George Smathers (D-FL), a committed internationalist, came down on the side of the State Department, arguing that hemispheric security was at stake.

Along one of the existing fault lines in the sugar universe, confectionery purchasers of sugar, accounting for about two-thirds of domestic use, were complaining about having to pay a higher price. Adding to the cacophony of the moment, domestic producers were citing declining sugar consumption in the United States as saccharin became the coffee sweetener of choice.

Finally, Representative Harold Cooley (D–NC), head of the House Agricultural Committee, forced a bill to the floor where it passed and was signed into law in May 1956. It extended the Cuban base quota but severely cut back on the island's share of, and possible growth from, either deficits or consumption increases from 98.6% to 43.2% in the first year and then down to 29.6% thereafter.

Batista, hearing ominous rumblings from the

Oriente province, became concerned about his future. He met with Eisenhower in Panama City in July 1956. He reminded the president that sugar accounted for 87% of his country's exports and that if the U.S. persisted in reducing its commitments that he would be forced to look for alternative buyers. The president demurred and in 1957, Batista made a deal to sell 150,000 tons of molasses to Russia, thus opening up a channel of both trade and communication to America's sworn cold war enemy. The communist party had been outlawed in Cuba, but with the sugar deal the door was opened a crack allowing the Russian bear to insert its nose.

Eisenhower had to act. He sent William Pawley, an investor in Cuba and friend of CIA Director Allen Dulles, to Havana with the strong message that Batista should step down to allow the U.S. to engineer a friendly military junta takeover of the country's government. Batista demurred, failing to get a commitment that he could immigrate to Florida with his ill-gotten fortune, and left the country on January 1, 1959, for the Dominican Republic, after Che Guevara's forces defeated the army at the Battle of Santa Clara. Eight days later, Fidel Castro, with his ragged band of revolutionaries, entered Havana and took power. Guevara was a dedicated Marxist and anti-imperialist implacably opposed to any American presence in Cuba. It was reported he spent his spare time in the sugar fields, "on the knife" cutting cane, to demonstrate his solidarity with the workers.

CASTRO

Once in power, Castro faced a dilemma. Cuba's export economy was based on a monoculture of sugar, with rum and cigars a distant second and third. The island was known for its flashy shows and magnificent casinos supporting a vibrant tourist industry—anathema to the new regime. To broaden the export base was nearly impossible with limited natural resources and to continue to attract tourists to the flesh pots and gaming tables of Havana was philosophically repugnant. With limited choices, Castro approached the United States with the request that it move the quota from three million to eight million tons. Rebuffed, he then decided to flood the world market with sugar to drive the price down.

Eisenhower was aghast and Congress, egged on by the domestic industry, passed a law giving the president immediate and unlimited power to alter the Cuban quota. Realizing that sugar was the economic lever to choke down the economy and perhaps creating sufficient instability leading to a coup, the president effectively set the 1960 quota at zero and decided to break off diplomatic relations with the Castro regime.[56]

By 1961, sugar had become a central element in the Cold War. By shutting down all Cuban imports, against the advice of his State Department, Eisenhower had given China and Russia the opportunity to step into the breach, which they quickly did. Encouraged by success in Cuba, and with plans to extend influence in South America and to create pressure to allow West Berlin to be given over to the Soviets, in October 1962 Nikita Khrushchev convinced Fidel Castro to allow medium-range ballistic missiles onto the island that could strike both Washington and New York resulting in thirteen days of a tense standoff between the world's two nuclear powers.[57] Castro was still seething over the failed Bay of Pigs invasion by paramilitary forces backed by the United States and saw this as a way to sever all relations with his country's neighbor to the north.

With Cuba imports out of the picture, the sugar barons saw the quota merry-go-round slowing and grabbed the brass ring. Florida cane growers and beet farmers in the upper Midwest wanted large increases in acreage authorized and further assurances that new mills would have adequate raw materials to keep them up and running twenty-four hours a day. But their message was muted by the fact that the world was being suffocated with sugar. Russian beet sugar had taken over leadership in production. In the U.S., the world's largest consumer, use of beet and cane sugar was being threatened by newly discovered near substitutes available at a lower cost to soft drink companies and candy makers.

The system in place for decades was falling apart. Tariffs became less important than quotas in maintaining price stability. Cuba, always the buffer to manage the level of available supplies making up for deficits was gone. In 1959, it accounted for one-third of the nation's needs with domestic beets accounting for 25%, Puerto Rican and

Hawaiian cane for 20% and Louisiana and Florida cane for 7%, with the balance from the Philippines. But the real truth, known to the USDA, was that beet sugar was not price competitive in the world market, and that given free and open trade without quotas and tariffs, cane sugar could be grown and refined at a lower cost to quickly dominate the market. The problem in the U.S., of course, was that political power resided mainly in the beet producing states. The result was that the American consumer paid more for refined sugar than if free market cane been readily available, and this was becoming more widely unpopular.[58]

FREE-FOR-ALL

The domestic sugar industry knew that existing laws would have to be changed which set off a war with different opponents in each battle. The first was the administration, represented by the USDA, pushing back against the aggressive sugar industry seeking higher domestic allotments. That was followed by a struggle between Western states beet interests and the cane sugar producers of Louisiana and Florida reflected as rural cane growers in the agrarian South versus thousands of small beet farmers in the upper Midwest. The third simmering controversy was considerable tension building in the state of Florida as "new" growers, mainly expatriates fleeing the Castro regime, began to buy up land and move processing equipment from the island to the mainland to compete with the "old" existing growers and processors. And in the middle were the refiners, based generally on the two coasts, accustomed to buying lower cost imported raw sugar and resisting any attempt to force the price higher. Finally, Florida was attempting to gain quota and acreage allotments against Louisiana.

And in the middle of the controversies, holding the ultimate hammer was a graduate of Yale Law School, "The Sugar King" Harold Cooley, chairman of the House Agricultural Committee, a man who knew how to use the power of office and relished the opportunity.

SUGAR AS FOREIGN POLICY

To bring order out of chaos, Cooley's committee called for an analysis of the world sugar market in 1961. Called the "Special Study on Sugar" the report stated that there was no free world market for sugar due to strict import controls by consuming countries and government subsidies in cane-growing countries. The U.S., to satisfy multiple interests ranging from the cane and beet farmers to the consumer, had used supply-side management to control the price, with Cuba as the buffer as well as unused domestic capacity, particularly in Florida south of Lake Okeechobee, which once properly drained could be quickly activated to fill the gap.

The Kennedy administration, with support from the State Department, had another take on the situation. With Cuba falling to a radical regime hostile to U.S. interests, the administration's theory was that by spreading Cuba's quota among other Caribbean nations, the action would spur their economies and subdue any civil unrest. Any new legislation should move toward something more appropriate to the world engulfed in a Cold War. One way to do this was to establish a global quota and, rather than identifying individual countries, allow competitive bidding to determine U.S. purchases. Underlying this was the assumption that cane-growing countries in the Caribbean, with low transportation costs to the U.S., would be the most likely low bidders and thus exporters.

Harold Cooley, getting a whiff of this tack by the administration, responded quickly and decisively asserting in a letter to the USDA that any departure from the fixed quota system in effect would not pass his committee and "that preference be given to those countries which offer to buy a reasonable quantity of United States agricultural commodities in return for our purchase of their sugar." [59]

BEET VS CANE

With the entire quota system under review by both the executive and legislative branches, beet growers and cane growers each saw an opening to increase their respective share of the market.

With the Cuban quota unfilled in 1960, and no reassignment of the tonnage, Florida became the focal point for new investment. The state had a history of land boom and bust, accompanied by the hyperbole of a carnival barker when Farris Bryant, running successfully for governor, boasted that Florida unfettered could triple its production in a single year. Land prices for muck acreage south of Lake Okeechobee doubled in eighteen months.

Looking at the boom cycle in Florida from two thousand miles away, Representative Montoya (D-NM) wrote to an official in the USDA complaining about the focus on Florida:

> "I have just read an article concerning the vast acreage in Florida which is presently being planted to sugar cane. I feel that the assignment of additional cane acreage at this time circumvents the intent of Congress. I am sure that you are aware of my strong efforts to obtain sugar beet acreage for the southwestern section of our country, but to little avail. I would certainly be interested in learning how these help Florida under sugar cane cultivation." [60]

Part of the unspoken strategy in promoting Florida's potential for growing and processing sugar was the expectation that once new quotas were announced, the Secretary could not ignore the tremendous increase taking place in Florida's sugar industry infrastructure. And these improvements to capacity were being financed from two sources: outside capital mainly from New York and money coming from Cuban expatriates.

Beet growers, on the other hand, were accustomed to having their own way in Washington. With two senators from each state, rural interests had an impact beyond the power of Louisiana and Florida delegations, and it all came pouring out in a Senate hearing of the Committee on Finance in May 1962, in a dialogue between Senator George Smathers of Florida and Senator Wallace Bennett of Utah:

"SENATOR BENNETT: The Senator is making the point that for a long time in the Congress there has been the feeling that beet sugar industry was a leech, a burden, on the sugar markets of the country, and I am proud of the producers in the West who have been attempting to slow down this price rise. They have supplied 200,000 tons beyond the requirements of their normal market, and they eventually had to follow the cane people whose prices are developed on the east out of the foreign markets because they could no longer have protected themselves." [61]

What was happening was that the "leeches" were receiving a lower price for their product than cane producers but kept their harvest within its normal geographic boundary. Western sugar rarely went to refiners east of the Mississippi River; the price in 1962 in Chicago west was 16.5¢ per pound for cane and 13.25¢ for beet. Bennett's comment exposed the underbelly of a schism that belied the appearance of solidarity.

Congress was stalled by the impasse between beet and cane. The beet industry wanted to extend marketing of their product produced in excess of the 1963 quota while cane sugar refiners, accustomed to processing less expensive imported sugar, wanted beet production reduced in 1964. The schism was open, obvious and would be settled by Secretary Freeman in favor of the Louisiana and Florida growers and processors. But before amplifying on that point, the swiftly changing dynamics in Florida needs context.

THE OLD ORDER BREAKS DOWN

In 1960, two corporations, United States Sugar Corporation and Okeelanta Sugar Company, controlled the majority of cane grown in south Florida, but soon new capital pouring in would cause a fracture between the "old" and the "new." U.S. Sugar Corporation (USSC) had dominated Everglades' sugar production since it was purchased by Stewart Mott in 1930. The Okeelanta Sugar Company had a different history, with its origins not in Detroit but in Puerto Rico.

The story starts with the South Porto Rico Sugar Company (SPRSC), incorporated in New Jersey in 1901 with $3 million in capital from New York bankers Muller, Schall & Company. Since Puerto Rico had become a territorial possession of the U.S. following the Spanish-American War, it was regarded as safe haven for investors anxious to cash in on the growing market for sugar. The company had a history of buying up competitors and in 1911 purchased over 20,000 acres in the Dominican Republic. Additional capital and management came from Germany and Henry Havemeyer, son of the Sugar Trust baron, was elected to the board in 1916.

Based in Guanica, a company town, the SPRSC operation was blessed with a deep water port and its mill by 1917 was second largest in the world. In that same year, the company ranked as 349 of the 500 largest U.S. industrials.[62] Fast forward to World War II: Florida's sugar industry was a virtual monopoly, and Florida's economic cheerleaders were concerned that the Congress and administration would look askance at increasing allotments to a single company, U.S. Sugar, despite the presence of one other large producer—the Fellsmere cooperative—which Frank Heiser had sold in 1943 to a group of Puerto Rican executives.

To combat the bad optics, the investor group, many of whom had experience with the SPRSC and Fellsmere moved a mill, piece by piece, from Vieques Island, off the coast of Puerto Rico, to South Bay in Palm Beach County, and began to produce a refined product in 1947.

Another corporation, the Okeelanta Sugar Refinery, Inc. was formed in 1952 by Cuban investors to buy up the assets of an existing mill. They expanded operations in 1959, escaping the Castro regime, and with the purchase of the Fellsmere mill unified all operations under a single umbrella, the Okeelanta Sugar Company (OSC). By 1959, those two main producers, USSC and OSC, were generating 160,000 tons of sugar, accounting for 60% of Florida's allotment.

The remaining 115,000 tons were being taken up by a number of other companies, all scrambling to get up and running to grab a piece of the Cuban quota. Henry Ford II was backing a group of Cuban exiles in forming the Talisman Sugar Corporation, and money was flowing into the Everglades like a summer thunderstorm, but there were already small farmers growing cane and they needed a facility to squeeze their harvest.

SUGAR CANE GROWERS COOPERATIVE OF FLORIDA

One of the most enduring expansion efforts of the era was creation of the Sugar Cane Growers Cooperative of Florida (SCGC). Row crop farming in the muck soil south of Lake Okeechobee had always been a good business but growing cane sugar was the most profitable. A celery farmer, George Wedgworth, gathered fifteen others to approach the USSC about buying harvested cane for processing. Rebuffed, they increased their membership and in 1960 chartered the cooperative for the purpose of building a processing mill, financed by an assessment on each ton harvested by co-op members, to handle the annual harvest of nearly 70,000 acres. With no experience in the manufacture of syrup and molasses, the co-op found what it most needed—a Cuban family with vast experience in processing and refining.

Wedgeworth was impressed with Alfonso Fanjul Sr. and his hands-on knowledge of the sugar business.

He provided the needed expertise as well as capital to construct a new mill named Glades Sugar House, up and running in 1962 with a capability of 6,000 tons per day. Management of the operation was contracted with the Czarnikow-Rionda Company, with a great-nephew of Manuel Rionda tied in with the Fanjul family by marriage, which took a 15% position in financing the mill.[63] That early friendship between Wedgworth and Fanjul would play out over the years, becoming stronger over time, leading to close coordination of the two business entities and eventually creating a working duopoly. And, it was an indication that USSC's domination of the sugar business in Florida was about to be challenged by the newcomers.

Displaced Cubans were moving quickly. Fanjul realized that with hundreds of thousands of acres available for raising cane sufficient processing capacity was necessary, and if USSC was going to process only its own crop more mills needed to be brought on-line. He had purchased 4,000 acres in Pahokee, just south of South Bay, the site of the OGPC mill moved from Vieques and began construction of another mill at Osceola with parts dissembled from three small mills in Louisiana. These were barged over to Florida to be put back together, striking concern in the Louisiana cane growers that their state might lose its position in domestic cane allotments. The mill, owned by Osceola Farms Company, cranked up in 1961. A second venture, called the New Hope Sugar Company, carried a corporate name reflective of the family's future in the United States which would later prove immensely profitable to the Fanjul family at the expense of the American consumer.

THE BUBBLE IS POPPED

Despite the scramble to build new capacity in Florida's sand and muck, the reality of politics, with the beet states still in control and the Louisiana interests maintaining their hardline position on new quotas, hit the state hard.

The Amendments of 1962 to previous legislation which had expired in June made important changes to the existing structure of the quota system begun in 1948. The Secretary of Agriculture was charged with the responsibility of comparing the price of raw sugar f.o.b. New York to the index of prices paid by farmers between 1956 and 1959, and to adjust quotas based upon a determination of how the new allocations would affect price.

Looking ahead, the second change was imposition of an import fee, or tariff, on sugar coming into the U.S. The price of sugar in the U.S. had been higher than the world price for years and the new fee began at 10% of the price in 1962, escalating to 30% by 1965. However, the new tariff system was never really tested because the world price of sugar in 1963 and 1964 was higher than anticipated and domestic producers were fully insulated.

A third feature of the amendments was that the substantial quota from the now discredited Cuba would have its share allotted pro rata among domestic and foreign producers.

Finally, the 1962 amendments designated six new acreage allotments for beet sugar, ranging from Presque Isle, Maine, to Mendota, California, and small additions to three areas served by new processing plants. The State of Florida was left out but had been tossed a bone when Cooley agreed to raise the mainland U.S. share of consumption quotas from 55% to 65%. The question was, of course, who got that increase.

Under the existing quota system, domestic production was estimated at 5,186,500 tons but then increased for 1962 to 5,810,000 tons. Beet was at 2,110,627 short tons but then upped to 2,650,000 short tons. Mainland U.S. cane producers were granted an increase from 649,640 tons to 895,000 while Hawaii, the Virgin Islands and Puerto Rice were all cut back slightly. Getting to the point where a bill made it out of Cooley's committee was not easy. Since sugar coming into the country was subject to an import fee, the amount allotted to domestic producers was a revenue issue where the House had jurisdiction.

When the dust cleared, the most obvious fault line, between the beet and cane interests, was settled in favor the former. It also exposed what was happening in Florida where speculative investment was rampant, Cuban families were buying up land and the politicians were incessantly arguing that the state could produce ten times its existing quota at an incomparable price—particularly when compared to beet sugar. Louisiana, the argument went, was disadvantaged in that it could not replant as efficiently as in the Everglades where damaged plants could be replaced in the same growing season, and besides the yield from Florida cane was twice per acre that of Louisiana.

Florida's arguments were not falling on deaf ears however, because from 1958 to 1963, Louisiana went from 240,000 acres under cultivation to 327,000, an increase of 35%. Florida had increased its acreage from a little under 36,000 to 139,000, an increase of 286%. With the world price of sugar high, up to over $8.00 per hundred pounds, the Kennedy administration was able, for the first time, to tie the domestic price to the world price, a move that would cast forever the future direction of sugar policy in the United States. But in 1963, it only drew the ire of everyone from soft drink makers to housewives, who complained bitterly about what they had to pay for a pound of sugar.

The beet industry on the other hand was pressing its case based upon an agronomic fact: beets could be planted on an annual basis whereas it took two years to get seed cane cultivars in the ground and grown ready for harvest.

The Kennedy administration's response to the turmoil was to require that the unfilled quota from Cuba (still technically in effect) come from offshore, mainly the Caribbean and South America for the sake of hemispheric stability, but as the world price accelerated that avenue was shut down by price competition from other countries, giving new hope to the beet and cane growers in the U.S. that they would be given large increases in their acreage allotments and quotas. Their hopes were bolstered by the fact that much of the world's beet sugar production came from Iron Curtain countries which would be off-limits for import, and the difference had to be made up from somewhere. Why not the U.S.?

For 1964, Agriculture Secretary Orville Freeman reduced the domestic quota to 5,700,832 tons from 5,703,463 in the previous year. Beet stayed stable at 2,698,590 but mainland cane went up to 1,009,873 from 911,410. Hawaii was flat; Puerto Rico, the Virgin Islands and the Philippines all got dramatic cuts.[64] Florida got the lion's share of the increase with small operations being favored.

TALISMAN AND THE ATLANTIC SUGAR ASSOCIATION

In an example of how small companies were coping with the chaotic situation, Cuban expertise was critical to Henry Ford's investment in the Talisman Sugar Company, formed in 1961 by Fernando de la Riva, the second largest grower in Cuba at the time of Castro's revolution.[65] He planted 13,000 acres in anticipation of Florida's being awarded a significant quota increase, but as time wore on, with no firm action from the USDA, the plantation ran into financial difficulties despite the fact that over a dozen of de la Riva's employees were involved in the Bay of Pigs fiasco supported covertly by the U.S. By 1963, Talisman was in financial straits, and had to cut back its planting schedule to 5,000 acres.

William Pawley stepped in. A close ally of President Eisenhower and Senator Holland, he had been sent to Cuba in 1959 to ask Batista to step down and was later involved in both the Bay of Pigs and Cuban missile crisis. Pawley used his political chips in a frustrated effort to get the government to clarify its position on future allotments. Secretary Freeman remained purposefully vague until April 1st, 1964, when he announced that only acreage planted prior to April 15th would be counted in calculating future allotments. Talisman was caught with its pants down. There was no way with only 5,000 acres planted by the deadline the company could sustain the $9 million capital investment already raised that contemplated clearing, dredging, planting and buying harvesting equipment for 25,000 acres. The Secretary eventually gave in and moved the deadline to May 1st, a grace period of only two weeks. Despite its travails, the company acquired the South Florida Sugar Corporation assets in 1964 from Puerto Rican investor Jacobo Cabassa, adding vast acreage to its holdings.

The April 15th deadline had been strongly supported by the American Cane Sugar League (all Louisiana growers) and some of the old-line companies in Florida because it would effectively shut out many of the new operations that had flooded the fields to take advantage of the Cuban embargo.

However the USDA and Secretary Freeman had a soft spot for the smaller farmers, represented by groups like the Atlantic Sugar Association (ASA), a co-op whose forty members had taken out loans from the Columbia Bank for Cooperatives in South Carolina and were partially backed by Allis Chalmers, hoping to demonstrate and sell their mechanical harvester. The ASA message was simple: little guys against the big guys. Freeman was sympathetic to the extent of allowing the Atlantic mill, which could not open until 1965, to count in its 1964 marketing allotment, thus giving it a pass on the restrictions in place against other companies.

The ASA continued until 2005 when it was merged into one of the Fanjul family holdings. Talisman was saved by Pawley who sold it in 1972 to the St. Joe Company, a large landholder and miner in northern Florida. It remained in operation until 1999 when sold to the government as part of an Everglades restoration project.

IMMOKALEE

In another case of smaller growers trying to get in on the frenzy of the moment, the Immokalee Sugar Growers Cooperative Association of Florida (ISGCA) represented a group of farmers, not in the muck south of Lake Okeechobee, but in the sandier soil west of the lake. Anxious to cash in on the high price of sugar, the situation was described in some detail by U.S. Secretary Orville Freeman in a letter to (then) Congressman Claude Pepper (D-FL):

"We understand that members of the Association have

planted 2,000 acres of 1964-crop sugarcane to be harvested as seed this fall. They plan to use this seed in the planting of about 33,000 of cane for sugar for 1965-crop harvest. They urge the department not to restrict plantings earlier than December 31, 1964, so that their acreage can be counted." [66]

What the Immokalee farmers were trying to do was beat the already announced May 1st deadline to determine acreage restrictions, and the 33,000 acres just happened to correspond precisely to a set-aside announced earlier for beet sugar to be grown in Presque Isle, Maine, beginning in 1966.

1965—The Pivot

By 1962, all parts of the domestic sugar industry were tightly managed by government regulation except for refiners and the frenetic purchase of land to grow sugarcane in Florida's Everglades. Unregulated and almost out of control were three elements contributing to the frenzy: farmers wanting to increase their acreage, speculators wanting to flip property for a quick buck (a standard business practice in Florida), and Cuban money and expertise escaping the Castro regime. Between 1961 and 1962 the sugarcane acreage available for planting in Florida doubled; cane acreage in Louisiana increased by 10%.

To reiterate in summary, the chaotic interplay of forces as set out in the last chapter, the 1962 farm bill amendments were in effect and scheduled to be reviewed in 1965. But the quota and allocation system was failing with Cuba no longer available as a buffer on the supply side. There was a question as to whether the government could maintain rigid allotments in view of the fluctuating dynamics of output, price and competition. Florida was on a fast track and in August 1962 the government gave in to the pressure. The USDA announced there would be no restrictions on the 1963 beet sugar crop, probably relating to Senator Bennett's comments about the beet sugar "leeches" receiving a lower price for their harvest. Then, in March 1963, all restrictions were lifted on both beet and cane allotments for 1964 for the continental U.S., Hawaii and Puerto Rico. How much of this was part of a government attempt to bring Cuba to its knees is not known, even today.

With the allotments lifted, bets in Florida were paying off. In 1964, the USDA reinstated quotas for 1965, but later upped the domestic allotment due to extreme weather conditions and a production shortfall from Cuba leading to a world-wide shortage. With its new capacity coming rapidly on-line, Florida's cane crop harvest increased 45% as compared to 10% for Louisiana.

CUBANS REDUX—FANJUL AND RIONDA

Part of the reason for Florida's rapid growth went back in time to the relationship between Cuban sugar interests and Florida. Similar in terms of climate, but not soil, much of the growth was taking place with investors who were supported by the agronomic knowledge and management expertise of expatriate Cubans.

American investment in Cuba took off after passage of the Platt Amendment and accelerated as World War I began. At the center of the action was the Fanjul family, having financed the Glades Sugar House in 1961, while taking an equity position, a move that started George Wedgworth on his career with the Sugar Cane Growers Cooperative of Florida. The Fanjul family's background is central to understanding how they came to be the largest sugar company operation in Florida.

One of the early family members was Manuel Rionda, a well-born Cuban who incorporated the Cuba Cane Sugar Company in New Jersey in 1915 while retaining 27% of the shares for himself. The DuPont family invested as did J. P. Morgan & Company and J. & W. Seligman Company, together accounting for another 30% of the outstanding shares. With this money behind him, Rionda had established his chops in the New York financial world and the company went on a buying spree, acquiring over a dozen smaller companies.

Rionda was based in New York, still very hands-on when it came to the Florida operations, running the Czarnikow-Rionda company which was at the time the second largest sugar brokerage in the world. He had begun work as a commission salesman for the Czarnikow firm in 1897. His two older brothers had built a powerful sugar and alcohol enterprise in Cuba, but both died the following year leaving Manuel in charge of the family's future. When Julius Czarnikow died in 1909, Rionda reorganized the brokerage to include his name but was always viewed with suspicion by the other partners in the firm.

By 1913, Cuba led the world in sugar exports and Czarnikow-Rionda was handling 60% of the sugar sales to the United States. The company had expanded horizontally into lending, insurance and administrative services to small growers and mills, snatching one up whenever the owners decided to sell through a subsidiary called the Cuban Trading Company. It even got into the wallboard business that had so interested Bror Dahlberg of the Celotex Corporation when he started the Southern Sugar Company in 1925 to use the bagasse for his fiberboard.

Rionda had been in the sugar business for thirty years and was blessed by the war in Europe driving the price of sugar on the world market through the roof. He also understood that bubbles eventually burst and was able to quickly move his finished product to market during the Dance of the Millions while his competitors were putting as much as they could into inventory waiting for the price to accelerate even further.

By 1929, Cuban sugar was competing with the tariff-protected U.S. territories of Hawaii, Puerto Rico and the Philippines and when the Great Depression hit was devastated by the protectionist impulse of the American government. The major holdings on the island were forced into bankruptcy and Cuba Cane Sugar was dissolved in 1938. But the brokerage survived and so did the Cuban Trading Company with its six mills; two members of the Fanjul family had served as presidents over the years.

The Fanjul family was related, by marriage, to the

Rionda's. Stretching back over one hundred years, Andres Gomez-Mena came from Spain to Cuba to make a fortune milling sugar cane. After he died in 1910, his son, Jose Gomez-Mena, merged the family's holdings into a single entity, the New Gomez-Mena Sugar Company, and in 1936 gave his daughter in marriage to Alfonso Fanjul, Sr., the great nephew of Manuel Rionda. When the two families took stock of their combined assets they owned ten mills, a large brokerage company, three distilleries, vast land holdings throughout Cuba and large parcels in Havana, all of which were nationalized by the Castro regime, forcing the family out of Cuba and into south Florida.

1965 ACT

New York and Cuban money were betting heavily on Florida being given a substantial increase in quota when the 1965 legislation was passed. In the four years from 1961–1964 acreage in the state had increased by 223,000 acres with eleven mills owned by seven different companies squeezing out 572,000 tons of raw sugar.[67]

Legislation passed in 1965 was complex and laden with political favors. One example of the latter was reservation of 10,000 tons for the Bahamas. The islands did not grow sugarcane at the time, but the Owens-Illinois Company with holdings in the islands and strategic political contributions, had made a deal to grow cane if the quota passed.[68]

Members of Congress and the USDA also knew that

speculation had pushed Florida beyond the normal range of expected growth, and that many companies were sitting on large surpluses. The U.S. price of sugar was also way above the world price at a 6.8¢ differential. Since foreign producers would get 35% of the estimated U.S. consumption, domestic companies would have to import foreign sugar at the U.S. price. The Senate's answer, pushed hard by the beet and sugar folks, was to raise the overall quota by 580,000 tons but to institute strict controls on acreage and marketing to work down excess inventory by controlling productive capacity.

The bill allowed the recently formed Atlantic Sugar Association an allotment at the 100% level of its surplus inventory and gave the same offer to Talisman and the South Florida Sugar Corporation. Three other Florida companies received allotments at a lower fraction of excess inventory: Glades County Sugar Growers Cooperative, Sugar Cane Growers Cooperative of Florida and Osceola Farms owned by the Fanjul family.

While a workout of the inventory was helpful, the new system added 400,000 tons for domestic cane sugar producers to 1,100,000. And Louisiana and Florida were each given about half of the additional cane allotment.

FLORIDA CATCHES UP

Looking back, two factors were driving Florida's growth at the time. The first was the sheer productivity of muck soil capable of producing a much higher sucrose yield than plants grown in Louisiana. Directly tied to that was a second factor—the influx of Cuban money and expertise in growing and processing. Aside from U.S. Sugar and the Okeelanta Sugar Company, smaller farmers had nowhere to go until Cuban money helped build more processing capacity into the system.

By 1966, there were 169 farms growing cane in Florida as against 2,080 farms in Louisiana, but the Florida output exceed its competitor state by 16% due mainly to the higher yield per acre. About half of the crop in each state was grown and sold by farmers independent of the large integrated corporations.[69] By comparison, and perhaps helpful in explaining the political power of the beet industry, there were 19,542 farms growing sugar beets in that same year.

While the cost of land, soil quality and preparation, labor costs of planting and harvesting were criteria for investors, yield of tons per acre harvested was an important data point as well. And Florida excelled when compared to its neighbor in the northern Gulf of Mexico.[70] For example, in 1966, Louisiana yield came out at 23.5 tons per acre while Florida yield was 32.1 tons. (The heavyweight was Hawaii, weighing in at 95.9 tons per acre.)

One result of the 1965 bill was to choke down growth of sugarcane speculation. It still occupied a second position: 1,100,000 tons quota compared to 3,025,000 tons for beet. But the 400,000 ton increase generated a great deal of confidence in Florida's future.

The decade between 1965 and 1974 was unremarkable as to any shifts of government policy. The sugar industry was consolidating in Florida, as small growers were either absorbed into co-ops or bought out by the large integrated firms. Price drove many decisions as farmers had multiple options as to what crops to grow in the rich, muck soil south of Lake Okeechobee.

The industry was also automating. Data specific to Florida is not available, but across the whole of domestic productivity man hours per ton of sugar harvested went from 28.6 in 1965 to 19.8 in 1973. Since almost all beet sugar has been planted and harvested mechanically since after World War II, it's likely that the higher productivity was mostly from Florida.

The number of farms decreased and the average harvested area per farm went from 228 to 460, a scale increase of nearly 50%. But the eye-popping number was the grower receipts per farm, rising from $45,000 in 1965 to $533,000 in 1974. Processor payments per ton of cane went from $8.62 per ton to $49 per ton in 1974/75 when world prices skyrocketed.[71]

Finally, the quality of cane grown in Florida increased dramatically. The true purity of sucrose is measured as a percent of dissolved solids in a liquid using a device called a saccharimeter which measures the amount of rotation of polarized light as it passes through a solution. The percentage generally varies from 96% to 98% sucrose. Research by the federal facility at Canal Point and state laboratories worked to develop disease-resistant and higher-yielding plants quickly adopted by farms in both muck and sand that maintained a high polarization.

HEALTH CONCERNS ELEVATED

While the sugar business was consolidating and expanding, medical research was becoming more public about its findings that sugar was having an effect on people's teeth. The Sugar Association, faced with bad press, was concerned that the government might regulate consumption and launched a counteroffensive against the mounting evidence.

Based upon available research, the U.S. National Institute of Dental Research (NIDR) began to work on a targeted research program to identify platforms for widespread application to eradicate dental caries (tooth decay) within a decade and in 1971, the NIDR launched the National Caries Program (NCP).

One eleven-member group, the Caries Task Force Steering Committee, influential in developing proper interventions to prevent tooth-decay, was populated by eight people sponsored by the International Sugar Research Foundation, a group extremely friendly to sugar. The guidelines, once issued, did not recommend reducing sugar intake. Instead, they turned to the use of fluoride and suggested that chemical additives could mitigate the effect of sugar on tooth decay.

The recommendations, with 78% lifted directly from

suggestions written by sugar lobbyists and consultants, proved ineffective over the ensuing years, and the NIDR suffered a loss of credibility as a result.[72] It was an example of how the industry, rather than just attacking from the flank, could work its way inside to neutralize criticism.

The debate over the health effects of sugar consumption was just beginning. It would amplify over the years and blossom into a full confrontation around the turn of the century when obesity and diabetes were recognized as major crises in America.

Roots of Modern Sugar Policy

As noted earlier, the sugar program in the United States was managed to varying degrees, using different mechanisms to control both price and quantity since 1890, with a significant strengthening of federal oversight during the Great Depression, with the Jones-Costigan Act of 1934 and with the foundational Sugar Act of 1948. Modifications to the program for the next twenty-five years were incremental.

Sugar legislation was due for renewal, but as the Congress convened in 1974, it was looking at another bubble. In January, prices began to escalate and the ensuing debate about the future of U.S. sugar policy became a central part of the legislative agenda in Washington, leading up the creation of the structure still in place today.

1974 – 1975

The world price of raw sugar blew through the roof in

1974 (cents per pound):

Quarter	World Price ¢	New York (duty paid)
Q1 1974	19.29	15.94
Q2 1974	23.03	22.87
Q3 1974	30.40	31.55
Q2 1974	47.26	47.62
Q1 1975	32.85	34.91
Q2 1975	18.42	20.43
Q3 1975	17.08	19.45
Q4 1975	13.59	15.09 [73]

In reviewing the situation in 1974, Congress simply allowed the existing governing legislation to expire. The sugar industry was comfortable until 1975 when prices began to drop precipitously. In response, President Gerald Ford, looking to be re-elected the next November, tripled the import tax on foreign sugar by executive order in the hope that he could win the State of Louisiana. He failed to do so and a peanut farmer named Jimmy Carter became president.

1977

President Carter, during his term, presided over a period of high interest rates and high inflation, characterized by Ian Macleod, a British Member of Parliament, as "stagflation." Sugar prices had retreated even further in 1976 and the following year Carter, at the suggestion of his Secretary of Agriculture Robert Bergland, a farmer from the beet growing state of Minnesota, directed the USDA to develop a direct payment program to sugar farmers.

The method proposed was fairly simple in theory. Processors would receive a subsidy of the difference between 13.5¢ per pound and the "national average price," with a collar of 2¢. So, if the general price was 11.75¢, a subsidy of 1.75¢ would be paid directly by the Agricultural Stabilization and Conservation Service (ACSC). To qualify, the processor would have to show "a written contract with each producer who had provided him with unprocessed sugar beets or sugarcane for the quarter."[74] After the payment was made, it would be remitted back to the farmer (producer) less any administrative expenses.

The authority for this was the Agricultural Act of 1949, passed to provide price supports for wool and rice at the time, but then extended to other agricultural commodities. Senator Wendell Anderson, a former governor of beet-growing Minnesota and professional hockey player, framed the issue by arguing that the 1949 law allowed payments:

"...if the price of an *unprocessed* commodity were supported by other means, the Secretary would have authority to make compensatory payments to processors to defray the expenses incurred by them in paying the support price, provided the market prices for the *processed* commodity were so low that the processors could not otherwise afford to pay the support price." [75]

The Department of Justice could not approve the program. While admitting that payments would "tend to stabilize the market inasmuch as they would encourage producers to stay in the market" the same result could be accomplished by payments directly to the producers. The final opinion was:

"We do not wish to suggest, however, that price supports to producers may never be provided by means of direct payment to processors, but if it is to be so provided, the processors must act as something more than forwarding agents for payments that are otherwise indistinguishable from production payments." [76]

The Congress, recognizing that the Carter/Bergland price support program was legally shaky, then made a slight modification that would underpin the sugar price support program in future years. Rather than making direct payments to processors, the Secretary could issue non-recourse loans taking sugar as collateral. If the market price was above the stipulated loan rate, sugar would be sold on the open market. If it fell below the loan rate, it could be purchased by the Commodity Credit Corporation (CCC) and the loan would be forgiven provided the processors guaranteed a minimum price to producers (farmers).

The main mechanism to keep the market price above the loan rate was through adjustment of import quotas, but the Carter administration was in the midst of negotiating an International Sugar Agreement (ISA). Setting a level of imports from South America at that time would be inimical to the government's position and undercut Carter's hope for greater flexibility and lower domestic prices. So, when the 1977 Food and Agriculture Act came to Carter's desk, the section on sugar was a brief three paragraph summary of alternatives available to the Secretary of Agriculture. The second paragraph read:

"The Secretary may suspend the sugar price support program when he determines the International Sugar Agreement (now being negotiated) is in effect which would maintain the U. S, raw sugar price of at least 13.5 cents per pound." [77]

When the ISA was finalized, ratification was immediately held up in both Congressional committees dealing with agriculture seeking a higher price for domestic sugar, Members in the Senate wanted 17¢ a pound and the House members were looking for 16¢. At the time, the world price was 9¢, and the administration's target price was 14.4¢. The break-even price at the time was somewhere around 13¢, so the padding being considered represented pure profit for sugar processors.

The back and forth had an ugly downside. Over two million tons of sugar was dumped on the U.S. market by foreign producers while legislative details were being worked out at a stately pace.

INTERNATIONAL SUGAR AGREEMENTS (ISA)

International Sugar Agreements hearken all the way back to the Chadbourne Plan of 1931 and were renewed in 1937, 1953, 1958 and 1968. They all had two purposes: first, to stabilize the world price of sugar and second, to ensure that production be equitably spread over time and geography. The oversight agency, the International Sugar Council, had survived World War II, but was hard put to maintain orderly markets during the Cold War.

As a general rule, people in business, both investors and operators, seek stability in price and predictability of output. An orderly market underlies the capitalist model, even if the market is tempered by government intervention and not ruled by nakedly open competition and free market principles. In the case of many commodities, the hand of government is visible and those who understand how the system works are able to extract significant profits from their knowledge. This applies in abundance to sugar.

In free-market economics there is a theory that nation-states can have either absolute advantage or comparative advantage in the production of certain goods and rendering of certain services.

Absolute advantage is where a given economic activity

uses fewer resources at a lower cost than any other nation-state. Comparative advantage is when a choice needs to be made as to what products in a nation-state's economic engine can be produced at the lowest opportunity cost when compared to other similar alternatives. And the utility of an international trade agreement allows production to be spread among multiple countries despite the possible absolute advantage of certain participants.

But sugar on the world stage is not a true free-market product. It is a state-supported commodity where most countries offer incentives, and in many cases direct subsidies, to stimulate and maintain supply. Cost becomes less relevant because it is subsidized by government payments. This last point was made by members of Congress and Florida Governor Bob Graham as they pushed back on the Carter administration's participation in the ISA, arguing that the dumping of two million pounds of foreign sugar had caused the closing of nearly twenty mills throughout the country, many in Florida.[78]

Finally, Senator Frank Church (D-ID), chairman of the Senate Foreign Relations Committee, and President Carter reached agreement on a sugar loan rate of 15.8¢ per pound. The Senate ratified to ISA in 1980, but it never really took effect because the price of sugar on the world market was on the rise again, reaching 36.01¢ per pound by the fourth quarter of 1980, as compared to 7.41¢ for the fourth quarter of 1977 when the bill was passed and signed.

Unfortunately, by then a few of the smaller Florida

mills had closed, leaving standing the larger, well-capitalized companies to move into the quota vacuum left by the departed.

1977 BILL FORENSIC

Although it was effective for only a short period of time, the Food and Agriculture Act of 1977 firmly implanted the nonrecourse loan program into U.S. sugar policy in which the USDA grants discount loans at a predetermined price (the loan rate) and at below prevailing interest rates to domestic sugar processors on a non-recourse basis taking processed sugar as collateral. This meant that in a year when processors were unable to sell their entire inventory in the domestic market at the loan rate or above, the collateral would be accepted as payment on the loan (and interest). The sugar would then be turned into ethanol rather than being put back onto the market, because added supply would further depress the price. This method circumvented Justice Department objections to reliance on the 1949 Act and effectively created a permanent floor for sugar prices, a floor that could be raised given the political inclination with proper emoluments to campaign coffers.

In most farm programs, payments go directly to the producers (farmers) but with sugar it is directed to processors, chosen because cane is processed by converting it to raw sugar while beets are processed directly into refined sugar. Cane must then go through another step to be crystallized and made ready for market.

The language in the bill shows how this was accomplished:

"Sec. 902. Effective only with respect to the 1977 and 1978 crops of sugar beets and sugar cane, section 2012 of the Agricultural Act of 1949, is amended by—(1) striking out in the first sentence "honey, and milk" and inserting in lieu thereof the following: "honey, milk, sugar beets and sugar cane" and (2) adding at the end a new subsection (f) as follows: "(f) (1) The price of the 1977 and 1978 crops of sugar beets and sugar cane shall be supported through loans or purchases with respect to the processed products thereof at a level not in excess of 65 per centum nor less than 52.5 per centum of the of the parity price therefore: *Provided,* That the support level may in no event be less than 13.5 cents per pound raw sugar equivalent." [79]

By including sugar in with honey and milk, the price support program was rolled into the larger package of major farm commodities like wheat, corn, cotton and rice. It could be dealt with as part of every farm bill in the future rather than standing alone where it could become a tempting target for opponents. It would not eliminate the tense relationship between beet and cane, between domestic and foreign, between refiners and processors, or between Florida and Louisiana but once a concept is implanted in legislation, or an ongoing contract, it is devilishly hard to remove.

One other aspect of the 1977 bill was that the Secretary was given the express power to "establish minimum wage rates for agricultural employees engaged in the production of sugar." [80] Cesar Chavez and the United Farm Workers were active in the sugar fields during the 1970s, having filed lawsuits against the government for failing to enforce wage and hour standards. In addition, a U.S. Department of Labor study indicated that workers had, for years, been paid less than the required minimum wage. The industry responded with the argument that costs were escalating rapidly, squeezing profits and making the industry economically shaky.

Against the background of the labor situation, a struggle continued between sugar lobbyists pressing members of Congress to frame the situation as one of survival and the White House pushing back with domestic prices in mind, as the world price of sugar was rising, satiating the appetite of the industry temporarily.

As expressed in cents per pound, prices were fluctuating around the support level at the time:

Quarter	World Price ¢	New York Price (duty paid)
Q4 1977	7.41	10.80
Q1 1978	8.33	14.01
Q2 1978	7.38	13.71
Q3 1978	7.23	13.44
Q4 1978	8.32	14.55 [81]

The farm bill was signed into law on September 29, 1977. The effect of the loan rate set briefly at 13.5¢ per pound before the ISA rate of 15.8¢ went into effect can be seen in the chart with the Q1 1978 price rising 3.21¢ per pound to 14.01¢. However, given the ongoing ISA ratification debate, there was an escape clause in the bill allowing the Secretary to suspend the price support program if there was an international agreement in effect that guaranteed domestic processors a floor at the loan rate or higher.

Also, in the bill was a provision that "... (e)ffective only with respect to the 1977 and 1978 crops of sugar beets and sugar cane, the Agricultural Act of 1949, as amended, is amended..." clearly passing a message that the program would be reviewed for 1979 pending settlement of the ISA price. But by that time, the price was continuing to move upward and lobbying pressure from processors and producers diminished as they took advantage of market conditions.

Quarter	World Price ¢	New York Price (duty paid)
Q1 1979	8.09	15.16
Q2 1979	7.94	14.41
Q3 1979	9.09	15.83
Q4 1979	13.49	16.83
Q1 1980	20.13	21.84
Q2 1980	28.18	28.89

Table continued on next page

Continued from previous page

Quarter	World Price ¢	New York Price (duty paid)
Q3 1980	31.74	32.64
Q4 1980	36.01	37.09
Q1 1981	24.69	26.50
Q2 1981	16.44	18.76
Q3 1981	14.25	17.33
Q4 1981	12.36	16.34 [82]

The 1980 bubble was caused by a drought in Russia and a freeze in the Philippines, but as world production came back online, prices began to drop back, and the domestic industry started howling again for government price supports to be reinstated.

Finally, by rolling sugar into the omnibus farm bill, lobbying power was scaled up with the resources of the politically savvy American Farm Bureau, agro-industry companies in Florida and Louisiana, and beet growers from twelve states—all combining to gather together a bloc of Congressional votes that virtually guaranteed a rosy future for sugar.

BUILDING FOR THE FUTURE—
FARM BILL OF 1981

Hearings in House and Senate committees responsible for constructing terms of the Food and Agriculture Act of 1981 were contentious, heated and divisive along the normal fault lines within the domestic industry. In the fray were beet sugar interests in the North and West, cane growers and processors in Louisiana and Florida and refiners in the Northeast and Chicago, all with different criteria for business success. Besides, the price was declining and the industry was pressing for more protection.

Confectioners were caught between their desire to buy sugar at low prices while understanding the necessity of protecting farmers and processors from radical price swings, but sugar's vast profits in 1980 and early 1981 somewhat blunted the protectionist argument. Refiners testified before House and Senate committees that they were not insulated in any way from rising sugar prices by government programs and that competition from companies using lower-priced corn syrup was directly competitive with their product base.

Looking at the price history of recent years, one idea put forth was to adopt the ISA terms of the existing program, since sugar pricing was as much an international matter as one solely related to the domestic industry. This was quickly dismissed by the sugar industry, asserting that the commodity was heavily subsidized by governments in all sugar-producing countries creating an artificial cost structure and leading to manipulated pricing.

Another question was whether the program had any effect on taxpayers. A Congressman from Michigan, a big beet producing state, reminded the House committee holding hearings that "... the sugar loan program covering the 1977, 1978 and 1979 crops ended up with the government making a net profit of $40 million on the sale of forfeited sugar. . . ." [83]

To add to the cacophony, a group of Haitians, having come into the U.S. as refugees, sued the government for failing to require Florida sugar companies to give preference to them as domestic workers over cheaper foreign cane cutters (mainly from Jamaica).

Despite all the fuss, the 1981 bill was approved by Congress. It included the nonrecourse loan program for processors using sugar as collateral, purchase and resale of forfeited sugar and inclusion of sugar as a basic commodity to be dealt with in all subsequent omnibus farm bills.

The 1981 bill also attempted to deal with corn sweeteners that were beginning to make serious inroads into the sugar market. Price calculations had to go beyond the beet and cane industry alone. To do that, one new twist was introduction of a complicated method to calculate the loan rate called the market stabilization price (MSP) ". . . calculated by adding a transportation cost factor, handling cost factor, GSP tariff reduction factor, an interest factor, and an incentive factor for processors to sell in the market to the loan rate." [84] The idea was to create a price level that took into account all costs. If the price of raw sugar dropped below the MSP, the risk of forfeiture was high but by including a number of indirect costs, it would generate a rate that would discourage sale of sugar to the CCC.

The problem, as with most sugar legislation, was computation of costs. The transportation piece in the MSP was based on the "average shipping charges from Hawaii to U.S. ports north of Cape Hatteras, NC, so that the MSP will be high enough to cover the processing area with highest costs." [85] While this added complexity to the calculation of the loan rate, it did no damage to the sugar industry.

With campaign contributions liberally sprinkled around the halls of Congress, the price (loan rate) for cane-generated raw sugar was set at 16.75¢ per pound for 1981 through mid-year 1982, 17¢ for 1982 through mid-year 1983, 17.5¢ for balance of 1983, 17.75¢ for 1984 and 18¢ for 1985. The price for beet sugar would be set by the Secretary as being "fair and reasonable in relation to sugarcane." The program would expire and come up for renewal in four years. Sugar had won again.[86]

Quarter	World Price ¢	New York Price (tariff paid)
Q1 1982	12.43	17.69
Q2 1982	8.17	19.50
Q3 1982	6.84	21.83
Q4 1982	6.23	20.69
Q1 1983	6.19	21.62
Q2 1983	8.93	22.52
Q3 1983	10.17	22.28
Q4 1983	8.67	21.75 [87]

The difference between the loan rate and the New York price (actual price paid for cane sugar in the U.S.) was achieved by adding in the MSP. The cost of producing raw sugar according to the USDA was about 25¢ per pound for raw cane sugar and a penny less for beet including all costs including depreciation, amortization interest and farm overhead. Projections presented in Congressional hearings went as high as 35¢ per pound over the next four years.

TRQ

Despite multiple levers to stabilize sugar prices in the 1981 bill, the world price was dropping and the domestic market was reacting with confusion. President Ronald Reagan, known for his aversion to government intervention in private enterprise, was forced to create a country by country quota system for regulating sugar imports into the U.S. and, despite his carefully voiced objections, did so with Presidential Proclamation 4941. The idea was to replace the existing method of estimating imports at a macro level, by setting out a specified amount for each country, based upon the estimates of consumption that would stabilize the price of domestic sugar for consumers, refiners and confectioners. The program was initially well-received because it allowed sugar to be imported at the pegged U.S. price, but soon reviled by Caribbean countries because their quotas were lower.

Many of the smaller countries were severely impacted. The biggest hit was on the Dominican Republic where the Fanjul family had invested heavily. And, in the category of unintended consequences, the quota reduction cut against one of Reagan's programs—the Caribbean Basin Initiative (CBI). Designed to provide lower tariffs to countries that did not expropriate American properties and business, the CBI was a push-back against Cuba in an attempt to stabilize hemispheric economies and prevent armed revolt by Cuban and Russian-backed insurgents.

The system was institutionalized in the Food Security Act of 1985, but later modified by the terms of the General Agreement on Trade and Tariffs (GATT) in 1990 which forced reorganization into a two-tiered system called Tariff Rate Quota (TRQ) wherein lower tariffs applied to "in-quota" imports and higher tariffs to raw sugar coming into to country above the specifically stated amount allowed from each country. The GATT agreement did specify that the minimum imports into the U.S. from participating countries would be maintained at 1.256 million tons.

Quotas were initially set using a complicated formula but modified over time to conform to the terms of trade agreements such as the Uruguay Round (which created the World Trade Organization) and the North American Free Trade Agreement (NAFTA) both enacted in 1994.

REFINED SUGAR RE-EXPORT PROGRAM

Among the fault lines in the domestic sugar industry lay the differing objectives of processors/producers and refiners. As covered before, refiners were after the lowest cost sugar on the world market and objected vigorously to paying for domestic raw sugar, with the price propped up by government support.

To be successful, refiners needed to keep plants running at full capacity for as long as possible. Their large production facilities were not designed for start and stop operation, and the solution was creation of the Refined Sugar Re-export Program (RSRP) in 1983, under which licensed refiners were permitted to purchase raw sugar at the world market price, if they exported an equal amount of the refined product within ninety days.

A similar program for companies making products that contained sugar, but not of the refined variety, were allowed to purchase necessary amounts on the world market provided they exported a similar amount within eighteen months. This eliminated one of the major issues that had divided the interests of sugar users from processors and producers, since the beginning of the price support program.

FOOD SECURITY ACT OF 1985

The 1985 act strengthened the price support system. First, the Secretary of Agriculture was given the flexibility to increase the loan rate based upon an analysis of the costs of production from planting to processing. If the price did not increase, a report had to be filed with a House committee that justified keeping the loan rate at the prior year's level.

Second, any farmer as a result of a processor declaring insolvency or bankruptcy who failed to receive maximum benefits under the program would be paid directly by the CCC.

Lastly, the whole price support program was to be operated "...at no cost to the Federal Government by preventing the accumulation of sugar acquired by the CCC."[88] This last provision has been a provocative measure debated ever since it was memorialized in 1985, particularly as to the meaning of the word "cost," but was inserted because the Treasury had to spend $105 million to fund loan forfeitures from the 1984 crop, some $47 million of which went to Florida processors and producers.

This last modification brought up a host of questions about what the true cost of the sugar program was to the American economy as a whole, and to unpack this requires a detailed look at the industry and how it was structured in 1988/1989.

Snapshot of Sweetener Industry

With the provisions of non-recourse loans, tariff-rate import quotas and domestic marketing allotments in place by 1981, with modifications in 1985, the sugar price-support program was due for reauthorization in 1990. Small refinements would be made in later farm bills, but the major elements were in place. While the terms of government support would remain, the sugar industry would undergo major changes as it evolved into an agro-industrial empire.

Looking back over this time period, the last price bubble in sugar was in 1980. There was slight dip in 1987, but after that prices began to stabilize around the loan rate, and the industry took on a normalized cost profile.

With that in mind, it's worth stopping for a moment and studying the overall structure and microeconomics of the industry at a moment in time, 1988/1989, when all the pieces were in place to create a baseline for comparison as we chronicle Florida's ascendancy to become the main source of sucrose in America.

GROWERS

Looking back over the many experiments with growing sugarcane in Florida, one has to be struck by the persistence of entrepreneurs in battling drainage issues, inclement weather, disease and varieties of soil. The New Smyrna community and Fellsmere both had a vision of planned communities around the fields to serve business interests alongside human needs similar to the earlier *ingenios* system in Cuba, reflecting the idealism of men and women who sought to do good by integrating all business and social activities into a unified whole. But with erratic government support, beginning with tariffs, maintaining an adequate price to justify an adequate return on investment, the early experiments proved unsustainable.

With price support legislation, the number of producers and processors in Florida with its warm and fertile soil south of Lake Okeechobee grew rapidly once drainage issues were solved. In 1970, approximately 170,000 acres were under cultivation for cane sugar; by 1989 the number had increased to 404,000 acres. The number of farms growing cane was 121 with the average cultivation 2,920 acres per farm. This number had held relatively steady throughout the 1980s while the area under cultivation in each farm had increased by about 40%.[89] However, the three largest Florida producers, U.S.

Sugar Corporation, various Fanjul operations and the Sugar Cane Growers Cooperative of Florida accounted for nearly three-quarters of the harvested cane.

Federal and state support of Florida, with the introduction and continued funding of experimental stations, created plant hybrids adapted to the soils of south Florida which ranged from sand to organic muck. Research into the application of various mixes of fertilizer increased the yield of cane plants. The data gained from these institutions was public and widely shared among farmers and by 1989 the yield per acre of recovered sugar after grinding in Florida was 4.3 tons, up from 3.4 tons in 1979.[90]

PROCESSORS

Sugarcane processing mills needed to be located near the fields because sucrose content deteriorates quickly after harvest. If the field has been burned prior to harvest, the sucrose content is even further reduced by a delay in processing.

The number of mills nationally was dropping slowly. In 1950 there were eighty-five processing units throughout the country. That number dropped from forty-five in 1980/1981 to forty-one in 1988/1989, a year in which Florida had seven processing plants with a grinding capacity of about 15,000 tons per day, most located near or adjacent to the farm fields. The three largest plants had a throughput of 75% of the 1.5 million tons processed.

The U.S. Sugar Corporation had been building

infrastructure since 1930. It owned a short-line railroad, the South Central Florida Express, using twelve locomotives and over 800 specially designed cars to haul harvested cane over 300 miles of track to deliver cane cuttings to its mills and raw sugar to main-line railroad junctions for further distribution to refiners.[91] This was an example of operational integration that would drive unit costs down through economies of scale. The model was so successful that by 2002, 95% of all sugar operations in Florida were combined into grower/processor arrangements by either ownership or contract.

REFINERS

In 1988/1989 there were 13 active refineries in the U.S. The big producer, with plants in Baltimore, Boston, New York and Chalmette, Louisiana was Domino Sugar owned by Amstar Corporation, the successor to American Sugar Refining Company started by the Havemeyer family back in the days of the Sugar Trust. The brand name Domino went back to 1901 when the company was refining over 1,200 tons of sugar a day, and by 1989 it had been bought and sold multiple times and was in the hands of Tate & Lyle plc, a British company. Other refiners were located in Texas, Yonkers in New York, Georgia and Florida. Taken together they could melt 22,400 short tons a day, way down from 30,760 tons in 1982 when there were 23 refineries.[92]

That was bad for the refiners, but good for domestic sugar processors and producers. In Florida, there were two mills, one in Clewiston and the other in South Bay. They had a combined capacity of 1,250 tons per day—about 6% of the total U.S. processing at that time.[93]

The trajectory of the independent refining industry was writ large and would continue on a decline in the future. The RSRP (re-export program operated by the USDA) was allowing about 600,000 tons of imported sugar to come in with low fees, but competition in the refined product was growing—from both Mexico and the Caribbean.

Refiners had always been second-class citizens when it came to legislative clout in Congress. They were spread over relatively few states and were highly automated so employment was minimal, and the economic impact of a plant closing had little effect on the national scale. Refining cane cost about three cents more than beet which did not need the added step to reach the crystallized state. In addition, the profit margin between raw and refined was less than one cent per pound in 1988, so refiners were paying almost as much for raw sugar as they could charge for the refined product and unable to cover all their costs.

Finally, there was an inverse relationship between the beet harvest and the price of refined sugar. Price movement also tends to be highly variable, adding to the element of risk for financial investors. This was illustrated by the fact that Amstar and Domino were acquired by Kohlberg, Kravis Roberts (a private equity and strategic investments firm) in 1983, sold to Merrill Lynch in 1986, and then to Tate & Lyle in 1988.

It would be sold again in 2001 to American Sugar Refining (ASR) owned jointly by the Fanjul family and Sugar Cane Growers Cooperative of Florida, leaving the venture capital world looking to maximize financial gain, and returning as part of vertical integration into a company, with existing growing and processing operations. The interests of refiners, for lower priced raw sugar, were historically set against the processors and producers. However, as vertical integration occurred in the case of the Amstar acquisition by ASR, the situation became increasingly complex and difficult for the government to manage.

HFCS—A BLACK SWAN

A major brake on the growth of the cane and beet sugar industry was high fructose corn syrup. HFCS is 76% carbohydrates and 24% water. By comparison, raw fruits like apples and grapes have about 5 to 10% fructose whereas dried fruits have about 50%.[94] In 1957, two scientists discovered an enzyme that would convert glucose to fructose, but the process was not widely adopted until the early 1970s. To the human sensory system, it is very sweet and is highly transportable in liquid form. That initially limited its use in some food products but would eventually be overcome as a low-cost crystallized fructose product was in the works.

HFCS comes in a number of grades ranging from HFCS-42 to HFCS-90. Milling of corn produces a number of chemical derivatives including ethanol. To produce HFCS, corn starch is converted to syrup that is almost all dextrose. Enzymes are then introduced to isomerize the dextrose; the result is 42% fructose. At this level, the syrup is used for yogurt, cereals, bakery products and confectioners treats.

To achieve a higher level of fructose, another pass is made through an ion-exchange system that keeps the fructose at nearly 90%. It is then blended into HFCS-42 to produce HFCS-55 for the soft-drink industry.

Coming into general use in 1977, HFCS rapidly displaced cane and beet sugar, growing at a rate of 600,000 tons per year from 1980 to 1985.[95] By 1990, it accounted for 45% of the added sugar consumed in the United States, a remarkable run in a very short period of time. Americans were consuming 37.5 pounds a year. In the 1988/1989 period, prices for HFCS-42 were swinging widely from 11.04¢ per pound in January 1988 to as high as 22.94¢ in September 1989. At its peak in 1999, domestic production amounted to 9.5 million tons.

One of the driving forces at the time was an emphasis on a high carbohydrate, low-fat diet. With proper exercise, it was supposed to result in weight loss, but was later discredited when the wrong kind of carbohydrates, mainly sugar added to refined products, were found to create inflammation.[96] While it closely resembled cane and beet sugar chemically, there was one small but significant difference that led to carbonyl and oxidative stress between fructose in raw sugar and in HFCS. When the debate about the effect of sugar on human health heated up, corn syrup became the center of attention, leading health researchers to point a finger at the primary culprit in the growing epidemic of obesity and type 2 diabetes.

SHOW ME THE MONEY

With HFCS coming into the market at a significantly lower price, cane and beet growers were at a clear economic disadvantage. For sugar cane growers, fixed costs varied little over time being mainly general farm overhead. The variable costs of planting, cultivation, harvesting, machinery operations and field services varied somewhat with labor costs comprising the main element. Processing costs included transportation, mill operations and marketing while refining costs are mainly in labor and transportation.

There was no way sugar could compete on a price basis with HFCS, running around 12¢ per pound as it ramped up production in the late 1970s and early 1980s. Farmers in the U.S. had the right hybrids and technology to grow corn in massive quantities, and the cane and beet interests were forced to look hard at their costs.

USDA COST STUDIES OVER TIME

In 1982, the USDA did a study based on data gathered worldwide from Landell Mills Commodities Studies, Ltd. (LMC), a British company well known to the American sugar industry. It divided costs into three categories: field costs which included soil preparation, planting, fertilizing, harvesting and transportation to the mill; factory costs including preparation, processing and storage of raw sugar into bulk facilities; administrative costs including management, depreciation of equipment, property taxes and other expenses not tied to the growing and processing.

The conclusion was that production and processing costs in the U.S. ranged from 17.97¢ per pound in 1979 to 21.31¢ per pound in 1982. The loan rate for 1982 was 17¢ per pound, so one might wonder whether there was any profit in growing cane sugar in Florida or anywhere else in the United States.

However, the New York price during this period ranged from 15.16¢ in the first quarter of 1979 to as high as 37.09¢ in the fourth quarter of 1980. The world price went from 8.09¢ to 36.01¢ for the comparable quarters. The wide variability related mainly to the fact that all major sugar-producing countries heavily subsidized their growers and processors, so the incentive was always to produce as much sugar as possible and dump it on the world market. Few countries other than the U.S. had a sophisticated reporting system, so growers made decisions depending on the current price although their crop harvest lagged (in the case of cane) by as much as two years given the time for cultivars to mature ready for harvest.

When looking at the cost structure, administration in the Landell Mills model was as much as 25% of the combined field and factory costs. If that was the case, variable costs were significantly lower. Using the 1982 estimate of 21.31¢ that would compute out to a variable cost of 15.98¢, well below the existing loan rate.

In another study, the USDA estimated that the cost of a 1988/1989 harvested crop in Florida was 13.21¢ per pound and 10.71¢ in Louisiana for 96-degree polarization raw sugar. Processing costs in Florida were 6.29¢ per pound for a raw sugar total of 19.50¢ per pound. However, these were only estimates; accurate grower and processor historical data was not available.

In 1992, the USDA did a further analysis of the cost of producing a pound of raw sugar, estimating it at 18.8¢ per pound in Florida. Taking into account cost reductions from 1979 to 1989 and all the data available, it would seem that the total cost was close to 18¢. This was later confirmed indirectly by To Dominicis, a vice president of Flo-Sun in an interview with Florida Trend magazine in 1995.[97]

Despite all the studies cited here, a true picture of the fixed and variable costs to grow and process and refine sugar in Florida was, and still is, opaque. There is simply no way to know how these are calculated internally. For example, the Economic Research Service of the USDA publishes a "Historical Costs and Returns" analysis but there is nothing in the data base about cane sugar.[98] The three major processors in Florida are all privately held, so there is no data available other than what they decide to put out for public consumption.

What is available, and instructive, are two studies done by the University of Florida's Institute of Food and

Agricultural Sciences, but even those lack real world numbers. The University admitted when attempting to obtain price information there was "...a lack of industry cooperation in providing trade information, this being due largely to industry consolidation and protection of proprietary information by larger producers."[99]

MODELING FINANCIAL RETURNS FOR TWO FLORIDA FARMS

With real-time data lacking, but using anecdotal information provided by growers, the University built theoretical models of two cane growing farms in Florida, each 5,000 acres in size, to study and compare revenues, cost structures and net returns. The first study was done in 2007 – 2008 for a "sand land cane" farm on mineral (sandy) soil similar to that found in eastern Hendry and Glades Counties. The bottom line for the year, net returns, was established at $131,000 or $42.74 per harvested acre.[100]

A second study, done a year later, for a muck soil farm located in the rich organic fields south of Lake Okeechobee, projected earnings of $1,351,492 or $343 per harvested acre.[101]

Deconstructing these two models provides some fascinating information about cane sugar farming in Florida.

First, the sucrose content from cane grown on mineral soil farms is higher than from muck cane, with a "quality factor" of 15.75% normal sucrose vs 14.5%

for cane harvested from organic soil.[102] The difference in productivity in the yield per acre was significantly different. The fertility of muck soil produced about 180,784 short tons vs 123,527 tons for sandy soil despite the models showing one small area of seed cane, one larger area of plant cane and three ratoon areas covering 4,100 acres for the muck soil farm and 4,375 planted acres for the mineral soil farm.

In the University's organic soil model, total per acre revenue from plant cane was $1,362, from the first ratoon $1,090, from the second and third ratoons $954 and $817 respectively. Overall costs per acre were $810 for muck and $1,024 for mineral. This would indicate that the muck fields producing the third ratoon were just above the break-even point.

Multiplying revenue per acre times the productivity of different fields, gross revenue was $4,545,872 for muck as against $3,276,497 for mineral. Multiplying the per acre cost by total acreage, both fallow and under cultivation, and adding in administrative overhead and bank interest at 7%, the models showed remarkably close total expenses: $3,184,380 for muck and $3,145,289 for mineral soil.

Another point is that interest charges in the 2008 – 2009 model totaled $84,038. A year earlier the 2007 – 2008 mineral model interest was estimated at $106,670, reflecting the recession during the time of the second study. It also highlighted the importance of interest rates on loans to processors being set at a very low level—well below the 7% used in the model.

The obvious conclusion was that organic soils south of Lake Okeechobee were much more profitable, and that in sugar farming the marginal rate of return on investment was extremely high. The world market price for sugar varies greatly, ranging from $2 per pound for raw sugar in 1969 up to $31 per pound at the peak of the 1974 bubble. Going back to the period of the university study, when compared to other crops in 2008 – 2009 wheat returned about $35 per acre, corn $198 and rice $55.[103] And while there is some variability in the market price of most domestic agricultural commodities, with sugar prices set by the government there is little fluctuation.

MUCK OR SAND

From the above modeling, one conclusion is quite clear. It's a lot better to grow sugarcane in muck than in sand.[104]

There are three different muck soils in south Florida, each depending upon the vegetation that formed the medium for crop growth. For example, Okeechobee muck is formed by custard apple leaves falling and deteriorating over centuries, mainly near the shores of Lake Okeechobee. Beneath the rich soil lies porous limestone and while the land is flat and not prone to erosion, it sinks into the karst. As it subsides, cane plants can no longer be held upright and the field is no longer suitable for growing cane. The current subsidence rate is about one inch per year (but varies by location).

The same problem exists in sandy soil where the mineral grains need to be large enough to support the height of the plants. Being devoid of any natural nutrients, it also requires heavy fertilization and requires almost three times as much phosphorous and other nutrients.

Sandy soil cane is a little sweeter but more difficult to manage. Muck soil can produce many more ratoons than sandy soil, so the costs of both fertilizing and re-planting account for most of the cost differential between the two. As mechanized harvesting becomes more popular, sand soil is more navigable for heavy machinery, but a little more abrasive on cutting blades.

For a mineral soil farmer, there is still a positive net return based on $42.74 per harvested acre or, translated into different terms, $26.24 per farm acre. Taken in terms of comparative advantage, or lost opportunity costs, these operations are marginal at best.

However, there may be other crops that could generate a higher return unless the farming operating is integrated into processing, known as "administrative cane." In that case, the lower return to the grower may be offset by profits from processing the cane into raw sugar. Part of the equation is mineral land available to the east of Lake Okeechobee. While it is somewhat more vulnerable to frost, it sells at a lower price. And, the land is suitable for crop rotation with corn and soybeans as principal alternatives.

Growing Opposition

Beginning in earnest in the 1980s, there was increasing pressure on cane growers in the Everglades Agricultural Area (EAA) to sell land in order to send clean water into Everglades National Park. For the three large growers in the EAA, there would be absolutely no reason to sell unless some external force intervened in their comfortable world of guaranteed profit.

The small, profitable and tightly controlled world of big sugar was coming under siege, but before turning to those elements of contention it is helpful to frame a broad-brush picture of the increasing scrutiny of the sugar program just before the dawn of the new millennium when Congress had become more conservative in its makeup and was taking a much harder line on all forms of government subsidies of industry and agriculture.

1990 FARM BILL

To add to sugar's growing external woes, federal debt was rising fast, and with the Food, Agriculture,

Conservation and Trade Act (FACT), it was clear that Congress was beginning to look hard at agricultural subsidies as a way of reducing federal expenditures. Newly inaugurated President George H. W. Bush had made a pledge to not raise taxes. The Government Accountability Office (GAO) issued a white paper mildly calling for sustainable agriculture and reductions in the price support system as a way to help balance the budget. The bill, once passed, did force some minor changes to subsidies for certain commodities, the main change being elimination of payments for taking land out of production and giving farmers more latitude in making decisions as to which crops to plant.

Sugar remained under the "no net cost" provisions of prior legislation. The Congress, rather than the Secretary of Agriculture, set the loan rate at 18¢ for cane and for beet at 22.9¢. The disparity between the two was derived from a complicated formula calculating full production costs between beet growers support levels and estimated cane processor levels.

Mandatory market allotments were discontinued unless the tariff-rate quota exceeded an "estimated" 1.25 million tons, at which time they would be reinstated giving farmers the opportunity to increase production. In 1988, imports had fallen below 1 million tons, but then during the inclement weather of 1990, had risen to 2 million tons, while the U.S. had grown its production from 6 million to over 7 million tons, illustrating the difficulty of balancing the need for imports and opening the old wound of refiners having to pay the domestic price, unless part of the Refined Sugar Re-export Program.

The attitude of Congress toward subsidies was hardening, but the marketplace for sweeteners was being altered by competition. There was an increase in the refining capacity of HFCS plants. With new investments in facilities, the amount of corn converted rose from approximately 320 million bushels in 1980 to 600 million bushels in 1990.[105] HFCS would peak at that point, but the use of low calorie sweeteners like aspartame was also growing, from 6 pounds per person in 1970 to 24 pounds in 1991.[106]

In an attempt to keep sugar prices from being further depressed by sweetener substitutes, and recognizing for the first time in a legislative package that economic alternatives to beet and cane sugar existed, the FACT bill set a 159,757 ton limit on crystallized fructose if the marketing allotments were in effect.

To tighten up the subsidy program even further, the market stabilization price (MSP) introduced in the 1981 Farm Bill, last used in September 1989, was eliminated. In addition, cane processors would be required to pay a 1¢ forfeiture penalty on tonnage purchased by the government. Beet processors would have to pay 1.07¢ per pound as a forfeiture penalty.

For the first time, a farm bill included a specific set-aside for environmental restoration of the Everglades.

The Secretary of Agriculture was authorized to spend $100 million, financed through either the sale or swap of federally owned land in Florida. It was also suggested in the bill that the money would be best used to purchase acreage in the Everglades Agricultural Area where nearly 300,000 acres were devoted, at the time, to growing sugarcane.

The FACT Act of 1990 was further modified later by the Omnibus Budget Reconciliation Act (OBRA) of 1993, an attempt to reduce federal subsidies by $3 billion over a five-year period. The centerpiece of OBRA was an increase in taxes on personal income in an attempt to get a balanced budget. The federal fuel tax was raised, the cap on Medicare tax was eliminated and a number of itemized deductions were phased out. The idea was to share the misery, so corn, rice, cotton and other commodities had changes made to the allotment and price support system. But sugar escaped.

With sugar being treated differently than most other farm commodities, public pressure grew to look at the sugar program with a higher level of granularity.

GAO REPORT 1993

Eyebrows were raised by the General Accounting Office in 1993. In a report requested by Representative Chuck Schumer (D-NY) in anticipation of the OBRA bill coming to the floor, the GAO found that the sugar program had cost about $1.4 billion borne by consumers over the past three years, and had primarily benefited only a small number of large, corporate sugar operations.[107]

Before release, the GAO report was reviewed in draft form by the USDA. Both the methodology and the source data were approved, adding to the credibility of the report. Authors of the report took a very conservative approach, acknowledging that the world price would increase if the U.S. purchased more sugar on the open market. Adjusting for those increases, the GAO estimated that $561 million a year, over the period 1989-1991, was paid annually by American consumers for the benefit of sugar farmers. Of that amount, 17 of 1,705, or 1% of sugarcane farms received 58% of the largesse coming from higher retail prices for sugar products. The split between processors and growers was assumed to be about 60 – 40, but the lack of hard industry data prevented a deeper analysis of the exact financial relationship because of the difficulty in breaking out numbers in the vertically integrated processor/producer operations.

Put another way, the study projected that 34% of the benefits went to farms with gross revenue in excess of $1 million. The estimated average benefit per unit for sugarcane operations in 1991 was $131,000 as a direct result of the U.S. sugar support program with its pegged prices.

The HFCS industry got a total benefit of $548 million. In 1990, four firms controlled 87% of domestic production, an indication of the oligopolistic nature of the HFCS business.

Another conclusion of the GAO report was that

"...the sugar program does not subject beneficiaries to payment limitations. For example, we estimate that one farm received over $30 million in benefits from the sugar program in 1991." [108]

Payment caps for other crops were first set out in the Farm Bill of 1981 to control the total cost of the farm subsidy program, but sugar at "no net cost" was never put under an umbrella of payment limitations so it was possible for large, highly integrated operations like U.S. Sugar Corporation and the Fanjul companies to receive large benefits with their economies of scale.

The last subject of the GAO report was a "by guess and by golly" stab at the profit generated from the highly controlled sugar program based upon data from the USDA. The cost of producing one pound of Florida raw cane for the period 1986 – 1990 was estimated at 19.07¢ per pound. The market price was 22.19¢—for a profit margin of 16.36%.

1996 FARM BILL

Known as the Federal Agriculture Improvement and Reform Act (FAIR), the 1996 bill emerged from one of the longest and most contentious debates in the history of farm legislation. Set to expire in 2002, it was designed to decouple farm prices and support payments, and to offer farmers more latitude in choosing what crops to plant and harvest, similar to provisions in the 1990 farm bill. The Republican Party had taken control of Congress and was eager to balance the budget. Agricultural subsidies were on the bubble.

Debate opened with an acrimonious attack on the sugar price support program by the Coalition to End Welfare for Big Sugar (CEWBS). The 1993 GAO report was held up as a government-sanctioned study critical of financial subsidies being shoveled in the direction of sugar. It gave purchase to groups opposed to the support program including environmentalists like Friends of the Everglades started by Marjory Stoneman Douglas, free enterprise proponents like the Cato Institute, and soft drink companies like Coca-Cola.

When the bill was being debated, the U.S. price was about 23¢ per pound and the world price 11¢ per pound. The House Agriculture Committee headed by Chairman Pat Roberts (R-KS) had been presented with the "Freedom to Farm Act," which would virtually eliminate all farm support programs dating back to the Jones-Costigan Act of 1934 and the Sugar Act of 1937, and allow the free market to set the price.

The sugar industry was appalled at the possibility of losing its preferred treatment in the pantheon of agriculture and turned a phalanx of lobbyists and lawyers loose. The result was a back-room deal with Representative Roberts to remove sugar from the "Freedom to Farm Act" and move it into the year-end budget in a "Christmas tree" bill. Cane and beet state politicians joined with peanut farmers to make the deal, and Roberts felt he had the votes to move the bill to the House floor. But unknown to him, cotton and rice interests had pressured committee members from their states to oppose the act, and it went down in a 27 – 22 vote.

The sugar industry, feeling it had at least blunted the opposition, remained determined to move its support program into the budget bill, arguing that with the "no net cost" provision sugar did not belong in a farm bill. The opposition, headed by CEWBS, was determined to keep sugar out of the budget bill, and to have another shot at it when a farm bill finally arrived on the House Floor.

Over in the Senate, the situation was not as dire. Senate Agriculture Committee Chairman Richard Lugar (R-IN) was a reformer but had only one Republican committee member vocally opposed to continuing the sugar program and that was Senator Rick Santorum (R-PA). Hershey Foods was one of his state's largest employers, but when the idea of modifying the sugar price support program arose he was quickly put in his place by Democrat committee members who were opposed to any changes and by other Republicans, many of whom were from beet and cane producing states. Added pressure came from Senate Majority Leader Bob Dole (R-KS) who was the beneficiary of large campaign contributions from Archer Daniels Midland Company, a major HFCS producer and at the time, under investigation for price-fixing. (The company later agreed to pay a fine of $100 million for criminal conduct—the largest antitrust fine in American history.)

The Senate bill attempted to reduce the loan rate

from 18¢ per pound to 17¢ but that failed in conference, so despite a powerful lobby and ample money sprinkled liberally around the halls of Congress, sugar stayed put in the farm bill. Non-recourse loans were continued, but only when tariff-rate quota imports exceeded 1.5 million tons. The "no net cost" provision remained and forfeiture penalties for collateralized sugar bought by the government stayed at 1¢ per pound for cane and 1.07¢ for beet.

In something of a reversal, marketing allotments for domestic sugar and crystalline fructose were repealed but the Secretary was given the power to restrict TRQ imports above the General Agreement of Trade and Tariffs (GATT) level of 1.5 million tons, all in an attempt to keep the domestic price well above the loan rate.

The contentious negotiations leading to the FAIR Bill of 1996 set the tone and aligned the forces for and against the sugar price support program in the future. Opponents published a newspaper called *The Bittersweet Times.* In it, one headline read "Aliens Earn Millions in Gov't Bonanza" referring to the Fanjul family who were described as "...non-U.S. Citizens [who] receive $65 million every year from the Gov't Sugar Program." One source described this level of attack by writing:

"... the discourse of national identity was now deployed against the Florida industry as opponents characterized it as greedy, foreign and un-American, overlooking the history of protectionism that had fostered the transition of U.S. sugar sourcing from Cuba to Florida." [109]

The overheated rhetoric tended to overwhelm the real issue in the debate leading up to passage which was whether or not the sugar price support program was working for the benefit, or to the detriment, of the American people. And much of that depended upon a full and complete picture of the damage to the public's health from overconsumption of all forms of sugar.

Sugar and Human Health

"The U.S. sugar program is a classic public choice case of concentrated benefits and dispersed costs; of how special interests can trump the public interest." [110]

It has been added to your breakfast cereal and yogurt, your lunchtime sandwich bread and Jif peanut butter, your dinnertime Amy's Organic Chunky Vegetable soup, Newman's Own pasta sauce and the al dente Barilla spaghetti it smothers. And, according to an article in the Journal of the American Medical Association (JAMA) it's not good for you: "Epidemiologic studies have suggested that higher intake of added sugar is associated with cardiovascular disease (CVD) risk factors." [111]

But Andy Briscoe disagreed. In a 2014 letter to an advisory committee of the Department of Health and Human Services and Department of Agriculture he wrote: "There is not a preponderance of scientific evidence for conclusion statements that link 'added sugars' intake to serious disease or negative health outcomes...." [112] Briscoe at the time was chief lobbyist in Washington D.C. for The Sugar Association, Inc.

Who should we believe?

HUMAN HEALTH ISSUES

Let's examine the evidence. Today, 43% of adults in the U.S. are obese, up from 36% just six years ago, with obesity defined as being thirty pounds over the normative weight for one's height. Nineteen percent of our children are obese. Airlines are redesigning seats for larger fannies; the U.S. Coast Guard has been forced to recalculate load factors for commercial watercraft based on new weight standards; and the U.S. Army is having trouble recruiting enough volunteers because so many applicants are overweight. One reason: In 1970, Americans ate 123 pounds of sugar a year; now it is 152 pounds.

The above are all symptoms of the major issue facing the sugar industry: in the past twenty years an increasing body of scientific evidence shows the negative impact of sugar consumption on the health of the U.S. population. The main areas of research: rapid increases in weight leading to obesity and type 2 diabetes, and the connection between excessive sugar consumption and cardiovascular disease.

SWEETNESS

After carbonation, pure sucrose is a disaccharide composed of two monosaccharides, glucose and fructose, making them available for energy when ingested. They are both simple sugars with the same basic molecular structure of $C_6H_{12}O_6$ whereas sucrose has a more complex structure of $C_{12}H_{22}O_{11}$. In layman's terms, table sugar is half fructose and half glucose.

Sweetness is sensed by over ten thousand receptors in the human mouth and tongue using a protein molecule. Originally it was thought that sugar craving was related to the body's need for energy, but more recent research indicates that the connection between the brain and nearly all parts of the digestive system react with pleasure to the taste of sugar. An additional reaction is increased appetite stimulated by endocannabinoids in the brain, the same chemical substance that reacts to THC in marijuana, which may make another connection to obesity through overeating beyond the metabolic conversion of fructose to fat.

Both glucose and fructose are carbohydrate building blocks. Once separated from sucrose by enzymes in the mouth and small intestine, they are absorbed into the bloodstream assisted by insulin. Glucose is absorbed more rapidly; fructose more slowly so it does not raise insulin levels as quickly.

When fructose is ingested, the human liver converts it to glucose—a more usable form of sugar for energy. The pancreas exudes insulin, which under normal circumstances allows glucose from the blood to be stored in the liver and muscles as glycogen. But when the human body is too heavily dosed with glycogen and if it either produces insufficient insulin or inadequate insulin, it converts the excess back to fructose and then to fat, believed to be a major contributor to the crisis in America today.

In 1957, Richard Marshall and Earl Kooi, two scientists working for the Corn Products Company, discovered an enzyme that could convert glucose to the highly soluble fructose from corn syrup. High fructose corn syrup began to slowly make inroads into the soft drink industry; from 105,000 tons in 1970 to 288,000 tons in 1975. But it really made its way into America's diet in 1977 after a series of punitive tariffs raised the cost of imported sugar for soft drink companies.

While quotas and forms of indirect subsidies for American beet and cane producers had kept the domestic price significantly above the world price, government subsidies for corn had also kept the price of that crop stable. But there was a differential, so soft drink and fast food processors found corn-syrup fructose to be a cheaper source of sweetener. The big two, Coca-Cola and Pepsi, both switched by 1984.

Both glucose and fructose are hard to crystallize but fructose, being highly water soluble, is perfect for sweet soft drinks. And, in its pure form it has a long, shelf life, defying crystallization and is able to keep food product such as cookies soft and mushy. The real value of fructose has always been in its sweetness. According to one source,

"It is far sweeter than glucose, the other component of table sugar. On a relative scale with the sweetness of table sugar marked as 100, glucose clocks in at 74, while fructose hits 173."[113]

HFCS AND HEALTH

Medical research began in the late 1970s with the introduction of high fructose corn syrup into soft drinks. The public was first made aware in a May 1977 article in the *New York Times* entitled "Sugar: Villain in Disguise." Using the best available scientific evidence, the author listed obesity, tooth decay, diabetes, and heart disease as possible outcomes from consuming too much sugar, but admitted that overeating, consumption of fats and the presence of cholesterol all contributed to the panoply of environmental diseases.

The same *New York Times* reporter, Jane Brody, followed up thirteen years later with an article outlining a Yale study that linked childhood behavioral issues with sugar intake. The study showed that after consuming sugary foods on an empty stomach that children became irritable, hyperactive and erratic in behavior due to a meteoric rise in adrenaline. Adults, given a similar diet, showed no effects.

By the year 2000, scientists believed they had sufficient data to identify the long-term effects of sugar consumption, particularly HFCS, on human health. In an article published in *The Lancet*, a widely-read journal of peer-reviewed science, they related sweetened soft drinks to the growing epidemic of childhood obesity.[114]

In 2007, another study of eleven carbonated soft drinks having HFCS by scientists at Rutgers University found:

> "... astonishingly high levels of reactive carbonyls in those beverages. These undesirable and highly reactive compounds associated with "unbound" fructose and glucose molecules are believed to cause tissue damage. ... By contrast, reactive carbonyls are not present in table sugar, whose glucose and fructose components are "bound" and chemically stable ..." [115]

The researchers went on to state that one can of soda contained five times the level of reactive carbonyls as compared to the normal concentration in the blood of an adult with diabetes.

Researchers were also beginning to suspect that the different metabolic process for fructose might be linked to inflammation and heart disease, but that connection developed slowly and cautiously over time as all good science does. The relationship with a high level of carbohydrates and coronary artery disease (CAD) is expressed in the following quote:

> "Diets with higher GL (glycemic load = rich in carbohydrates) and GI (glycemic index = rapidly absorbed

carbohydrates, predominantly soluble ones as in #1 above) are associated with ~ 2 times risk of CAD, especially in obese women. Correlation in men and thinner women is harder to prove.

"Diets with higher GI and GL are associated with increases in multiple CAD risk factors including obesity, abdominal obesity (metabolic syndrome or Syndrome X), hypertension, high total and LDL cholesterol, low HDL cholesterol, and higher measures of inflammation." [116]

IS ALL SUGAR BAD?

Back in the mid-seventies, the U.S. Food and Drug Administration (FDA) conducted a series of hearings to determine which foods were "generally recognized as safe." Two members of the review team had received money from the sugar industry to fund research projects, and in 1976 the FDA declared that sugar was not a public health hazard. Beyond the optics, there was a deeper implication: food and confectioner manufacturers could add any amount of sugar to any food.[117]

The report stimulated a torrent of opposition, and the government finally retreated into calling for a reduction in sugar consumption without any specific guidelines.

By 2002, the American Heart Association (AHA) was becoming less modest in its assessment of studies attempting to correlate sugar intake with a number of health problems which might extend into cardiovascular disease:

> "No data suggest that sugar intake per se is advantageous, and some data suggest it may be detrimental. The studies above, taken in total, indicate that high sugar intake should be avoided. Sugar has no nutritional value other than to provide calories." [118]

A second scientific shoe dropped when the World Health Organization (WHO) came out with a 2003 recommendation that no more than 10% of daily calories should come from sugar. The Sugar Association, formed by the industry to present sugar as a beneficial part of daily diets went on the attack, attempting to cancel WHO funding by the Congress and insisting that the Secretary of Health and Human Services, Tommy Thompson, force WHO to withdraw its report. Eventually, WHO did withdraw its recommendation, after being blistered by the sugar and confectioner industries.

Articles in a highly respected journal like *The Lancet* and recommendations from WHO had some impact but the heaviest blow came from a government report issued by the combined U.S. Department of Health and Human Services and Department of Agriculture, that bluntly linked sugar-loaded drinks with obesity and recommended consumption levels even lower than WHO, at no more than eight teaspoons per day.

The government report was followed up by a 2009 recommendation from the AHA that women consume no more than six teaspoons a day and men no more than nine teaspoons a day. At the time, the U.S. consumption rate was twenty-two teaspoons per day. By comparison a 12-ounce Coca-Cola contains about twelve teaspoons of sugar, so under the guidelines a woman should be drinking only one 6-ounce Coke per day.[119]

For years, obesity was believed to be the main cause of type 2 diabetes but a batch of new studies related excess sugar consumption directly to the disease. In March 2013, the open-access scientific journal PLOS ONE published a peer-reviewed study from the University of California San Francisco isolating the link between high sugar consumption and type 2 diabetes (after adjusting for other factors such as obesity).[120]

A study done by George Bray, head of Louisiana State University's Biomedical Research Center concluded that "...the increase in consumption of HFCS has a temporal relation to the epidemic of obesity, and the overconsumption of HFCS in calorically sweetened beverages may play a role in the epidemic of obesity." [121]

Another study done in 2010 by the same lead author linked the consumption of soft drinks with obesity throughout all age groups. It concluded that "...on the basis of data assembled here that in the amounts currently consumed, fructose is hazardous to the cardiometabolic health of many children, adolescents and adults." [122]

In addition to obesity and type 2 diabetes, the AHA bluntly stated that high added sugar consumption caused a variety of other medical conditions—including high blood pressure, heart disease and stroke. In a study published in 2014 in *JAMA Internal Medicine*, Dr. Hu of Harvard and his colleagues found an association between a high-sugar diet and a greater risk of dying from heart disease. Over the course of the 15-year study, people who got 17% to 21% of their calories from added sugar had a 38% higher risk of dying from cardiovascular disease compared with those who consumed 8% of their calories as added sugar.[123]

The number of studies was by then in the tens of thousands, increasing as time passed, and the health of the American people growing older and living longer was coming under more scrutiny. As the evidence continued to accumulate on the effects of sugar, as well as fat, salt and insufficient exercise, the entire sugar industry was mobilized into a broad-based defense of its product.

INDUSTRY RESPONDS

As scientific evidence mounted, the sugar industry, headed by the Sugar Association Inc., responded in kind but started from a deficit position from an earlier misfire. It was discovered by the *New York Times* that the Sugar Research Foundation had paid to have a study done in the 1960s that shifted the blame for health issues afflicting the American public from sugar to fat:

"The documents show that a trade group called the Sugar Research Foundation, known today as the Sugar Association, paid three Harvard scientists the equivalent of about $50,000 in today's dollars to publish a 1967 review of research on sugar, fat and heart disease. The studies used in the review were handpicked by the sugar group, and the article, which was published in the prestigious *New England Journal of Medicine,* minimized the link between sugar and heart health and cast aspersions on the role of saturated fat." [124]

Beverage folks were doing much the same thing. The Coca-Cola Company had started a non-profit called Global Balance Energy Network whose mission was to distract attention from consumption of sugar-loaded, colored, fizzy water by placing the blame for obesity on a lack of exercise. In the effort, they enlisted a number of scientists, always for a fee, using social media and medical publications to get the message out. The *Times* reporter who covered the Sugar Research Foundation story involving the Harvard professors described the effort as follows:

"Funding from the food industry is not uncommon in scientific research. But studies suggest that the funds tend to bias findings. A recent analysis of beverage studies, published in the journal *PLoS Medicine,* found that those funded by

Coca-Cola, PepsiCo, the American Beverage Association and the sugar industry were five times more likely to find no link between sugary drinks and weight gain than studies whose authors reported no financial conflicts." [125]

To add to the background issue of questionable science, the Associated Press used a records request to uncover the facts behind a study funded by candy makers, including Hershey Foods, Butterfingers and Skittles that concluded children who ate candy weighed less than kids who did not. The study extracted data from a government compendium of surveys about what people ate in the preceding 24 hours. While the study asserted that the data "may not reflect usual intake" and that "cause and effect associations could not be drawn," it nonetheless asserted that young people who ate candy were less obese or overweight.[126]

The study's authors claimed that candy makers had no role in designing the study; however the National Confectioners Association (NCA) was given an early draft copy for review and comment. After a great deal of back and forth with the authors, the NCA boldly asserted that its review of the document had no impact upon the results of the study. The manuscript was judged to be acceptable and it was released.

Another way of making sugar's point was to directly confront the epidemiological studies. For example, John White, head of White Technical Research, in a paper titled

"Straight talk about high fructose corn syrup" directly referenced the argument set forth by Louisiana State University's George Bray:

> "The HFCS-obesity hypothesis of Bray *et al* relies heavily on the positive association between HFCS use and obesity rates in the United States. However, Bray *et al* treated this association in isolation, offering no perspective on trends in total caloric intake. . . ." [127]

White's firm as listed on LinkedIn notes that it has been "serving the food and beverage industry since 1994. . . ." [128]

BOTTOM LINE

A developing consensus among scientists about the public health threat posed by sugar-laden products, mainly HFCS, forced disparate factions within the industry to unite. To attack sugar as an unhealthy food engaged a much larger segment of American business than just the Florida growers and processors. The sugar producers had temporary allies in the sugar users because all were being attacked on the health front. And all were involved in a full-court press to maintain their place in the economy despite the increasingly dire warnings as to the effect of their products on the public. There was little coordination of efforts because each had a separate message to bring to the public. The two things they all agreed upon were the need to fight science with science, and that a firm, positive defense needed to be constructed in absolute terms avoiding any uncertainty.

Science is based upon uncertainty, upon questioning and upon the painful road of testing and tweaking hypotheses until some semblance of agreement takes place. And Americans do not like uncertainty; it's not our cultural DNA. An example of science at work is apparent in another recent study by Canadian scientists to determine if there was a definite connection between fructose and diabetes. They could find none in the cohort study and the group concluded thus:

"Our systematic review and meta-analysis of available prospective cohort studies does not support an adverse association between intake of fructose-containing sugars independent of food form and risk of type 2 diabetes. Our confidence in the evidence for this conclusion is generally weak." [129]

As a people, we respect honesty, and while there is always a degree of uncertainty as expressed in the above quote it does not qualify as opposition research. It is just science at work, constantly questioning.

Much like the tobacco industry in the 1970s when growing evidence about the hazards of smoking was grinding into America's collective conscience, the sugar industry has relied upon special interest legislation, supported by elected officials in sugar-growing states.

And, taking a page from tobacco's play book, the industry gathered a few scientists to do studies disparaging links between added sugar consumption and human health problems. High fructose sugar became a convenient scapegoat for the obesity epidemic sweeping the country, but as some of the shadier aspects of opposition research began to leak out, it compromised the credibility of both the scientists involved and those companies funding the research in order to achieve a preconceived outcome.

Despite tap-dancing by a few scientists still willing to take sugar money, the preponderance of clinical research continues to build showing a clear connection between excessive sugar consumption and obesity, type 2 diabetes and cardiovascular disease in our country. The cost of obesity alone, according to the Harvard School of Public Health, is approximately $190 billion per year.

The sugar industry, like tobacco, can only hold off accumulating scientific evidence temporarily but as long as politicians are beholden to their sweet contributors the social and direct economic costs we all pay—much of which ends up in the pockets of the sugar barons—will continue.

The EAA

Despite repeating some slivers written in earlier chapters, it's helpful to review the history of Lake Okeechobee to establish context for the next few chapters at the beginning of an era of confrontation and litigation between sugar and Florida's growing environmental movement. As the English and Spanish traded ownership of Florida in the eighteenth century, their main interest was always along both coasts, but in the center of the state was the second largest body of fresh water fully enclosed in what would become the United States: Lake Okeechobee.

Named "Okeechobee" by the Seminoles (translated into English as "big water") it covered 730 sq. miles formed as a shallow depression and modified by sediment and erosion. It contained three islands protruding from the saucer-like lake bottom and owed its origins and replenishment to both heavy summer rains and the 4,500 sq. mile Kissimmee Lakes watershed beginning just south of the present city of Orlando.

To the south of the lake was a mass of muck, a large

swath of land, where water oozed, at the rate of one-half mile per day down into Florida Bay. Affectionately called the "The River of Grass" by Marjory Stoneman Douglas in her famous book of the same title, it was called Pa-hay-Okee by the indigenous people—which translated is "grassy waters."

As the Anglo-Europeans moved in, they regarded the continent as an opportunity to create a new Eden comprised of small farms growing enough food to feed the new nation—the vision of Thomas Jefferson. The Swamp and Overflowed Lands Act was passed by Congress in 1850, giving states the right to claim any land, in its natural state, unfit for agriculture. Florida, having been granted statehood only five years earlier, took full advantage, claiming 20 million acres as state lands.

Then, in 1855, the state created the Internal Improvement Fund (IIF), overseen by the governor and four members of the cabinet, to decide how to put the state lands to the best and highest use, a mantra to be repeated through the present day.

The IIF saw the fastest way to develop the state was to bring in railroads, but so much money and effort was being spent on opening the American west that the rail companies had little use for the mosquito-infested and hurricane-prone appendage occupying the country's southeastern corner.

In 1881, Philadelphia developer, Hamilton Disston, cut a deal for 4 million acres of swampland, for which he would drain another 12 million acres of state land. If successful, he would acquire one-half of the drained land—which happened to be part of the River of Grass—an area covered by rich muck ideal for farming.

The scheme never worked but was doubled down by Governor Napoleon Bonaparte Broward, and his "Empire of the Everglades." The project quickly ran out of money and Broward attempted to recover some of the losses by selling 500,000 acres to a developer. The price of land began to skyrocket, but reports also began to circulate that some of the drainage assumptions were wrong, leading the market to collapse followed by a series of lawsuits by buyers and their lawyers.

Despite all the excitement about development, farming had begun to take hold on a workable scale in sections where the drainage could be carried out easily and where water was abundant—around the southern border of Lake Okeechobee.

Sugar cane had been grown south of the lake since around 1890 and along the edge, where the oozing sediment hardened into marl that sealed the underlying porous limestone. A number of small towns appeared at the edge of the lake, towns like Clewiston and Belle Glade both founded in 1925, the same year that Bror Dahlberg started the Southern Sugar Company.

Then, in 1926, a hurricane hit south Florida and the dirt levee protecting Moore Haven, a city on the southwestern edge of the lake, was inundated as the partially completed canal system failed, the result of bad planning and execution. Four hundred souls lost their lives. Two years later, the same story repeated itself when in September 1928, another storm blasted through the state killing thousands. Many lived in the town of Belle Glade and were migrant workers brought in to till and harvest the crops being grown in the Everglades.

C&SF PROJECT

The devastation brought President Herbert Hoover, an engineer by training, to the scene. Promising it would never happen again, he got Congress to appropriate funds for the U.S. Army Corps of Engineers (USACE) to build an 85-mile dike along the southern edge of the lake. The original project would later grow into a 143-mile long levee surrounding much of the lake's perimeter.

The nation soon plunged into the Great Depression and while the urban population throughout the country was marginalized, farming operations south of Lake Okeechobee thrived. South Florida was spared serious hurricane damage for the next fifteen years but was plagued by droughts at the end of World War II.

That all changed with a vengeance when 1947 Miami recorded over 100 inches of rainfall, twice the annual average. The Hoover Dike held, but cities on the east coast were inundated, leading Congress to authorize the Corps to build the Central and South Florida Project for Flood Control and Other Purposes (C&SF). The magic words were "Other Purposes."

The project took twenty years to build out. It created a water management and control system that covered 15,000 square miles and eighteen counties in south Florida. Land was set aside for agriculture immediately south of the lake, known as the Everglades Agricultural Area (EAA) and the rich soil was perfect for growing lettuce, celery, radishes, beans and rice. The sugarcane growers, consisting of small farmers in the years before and immediately after the Hoover Dike was built, were well served by the project and able to sell their harvest to processors like the U.S. Sugar Corporation.

The year 1947 also saw publication of Marjory Stoneman Douglas' game-changing book: *The Everglades: River of Grass* with its lyrical opening paragraph:

> "There are no other Everglades in the world. They are, they have always been, one of the unique regions of the earth; remote, never wholly known. Nothing anywhere else is like them. . . ."

Douglas was a journalist at the *Miami Herald*, a newspaper owned by her father, and had intimate knowledge of the history of the region and a love of the landscape.

Until that time most people had regarded the Everglades as a worthless swamp converted to a potential agricultural paradise. Douglas' book was the opening shot in what would become all-out war between environmental organizations and agro-industrial operations in the EAA where growing both vegetables and sugar require nitrogen and phosphate. Douglas followed up two decades later by founding Friends of the Everglades, the first organization with a mission to restore the Everglades to as close to its systemic origins as possible.

Despite concern about destroying the ecosystem with hundreds of pumps and the lake nearby, the "Other Purposes" of promoting agriculture allowed Florida growers to operate year-round by moving water south to irrigate in the dry season, and back to the lake as a receptacle for back-pumped water when it was no longer needed.

Between 1960 and 1968, acreage used for growing sugarcane in the EAA quadrupled as the C&SF project continued to drain the land during the final years of the project.

Later, between 1973 and 1978, the amount of phosphorous runoff generated from both industrial farming operations in the EAA and cattle ranching and dairy cows feeding into the Kissimmee River watershed combined to double the amount of nitrogen and phosphorous in Lake Okeechobee. While some of the nutrient-laden water was sent down the St. Lucie to the Indian River Lagoon and the rest down the Caloosahatchee to be dumped into Charlotte Harbor, much of it remained in the lake, sinking slowly toward the bottom to create a hardening legacy that would haunt the lake and coastal estuaries in the years to come.

In summary, the 1947 C&SF project created a drainage and water management system south of the lake that led to intensified industrial agricultural operations in which the demand for water, both in and out of the fields on a timely basis, was deemed essential and available for crop growth and harvest. The inflow of nitrogen and phosphorous from the EAA, combined with cattle and dairy operations in the Kissimmee River watershed, eventually led to pollution of the lake where conditions were even more ideal for the growth of large colonies of cyanobacteria. The question then arose: who is responsible for the mess and who should pay for the cleanup?

TWO AGENCIES: WATER QUALITY AND WATER QUANTITY

State management of Lake Okeechobee was first put in place in 1949 by creation of the Central and South Florida Flood Control District as a modality of coordinating the state's effort with the federal C&SF project underway.

That was followed in 1972 by the establishment of five water management districts with passage of the Florida Water Resources Act, a brilliant piece of legislation that created five separate governmental entities based upon watersheds and not the normal geopolitical boundaries of counties and other jurisdictions. The lake was within the boundary of South Florida Water Management District (SFWMD). The district had a multiplicity of other responsibilities such as the issuance of consumptive use permits, approval of large development projects and the leasing of state-owned land to farms south of the lake, but most important was its critical function of assuring the quality of the water in the system was within federal and state guidelines.

A problem, not apparent from the beginning, was joint oversight of lake operations with the USACE. The quantity and timing of water releases to control the overall lake level was vested in the Corps, more specifically in something called the Lake Okeechobee Release Schedule (LORS) subject to periodic review and revision. The Corps was also part of the approval process for development plans, but control and timing of water coming out of the lake was critical over the ensuing years as the Hoover Dike began to weaken and possibly fail, flooding communities south of the lake.

This dual responsibility divided between two agencies, the SFWMD and USACE, would become entangled in a complex suit filed in 1988 by U.S. Attorney Dexter Lehtinen that brought out knives between Florida's sugar industry and some powerful environmental groups .

Knives Out

In the early years, right after completion of the C&SF project, with the beginning of large-scale faming in the EAA, the hostility between environmental advocates like Friends of the Everglades and the thriving sugar industry was somewhat suppressed. Disagreements were conducted with a level of civility using administrative agencies to adjudicate differences to avoid having to go to the courts. That was all about to end.

POLLUTION OF EVERGLADES NATIONAL PARK

Dexter Lehtinen was a savvy politician possessed of unlimited energy and a passion for the Everglades which he knew well having grown up in Homestead, Florida. After serving in U.S. Special Forces in the Vietnam War, he became a member of the Florida House. After one term, he moved to the state Senate, switched parties, to become a rising star in the Republican Party and was appointed by President Reagan's Justice Department in 1988 to the top law enforcement job in Miami.

Everglades National Park (ENP) at the time was suffering from overloads of phosphorous (P) and nitrogen (N) washing down through the EAA and into the park. In addition, canals in the Loxahatchee National Wildlife Preserve, adjacent to the EAA, were choked with cattails, a sure sign of excessive nutrients in the ecosystem. The SFWMD, tasked with regulating water quality in south Florida, had allowed runoff from the EAA to exceed 200 parts per billion (ppb) when the existing level in the park had once been 10 ppb before the C&SF project and before 700,000 acres of agricultural fields south of Lake Okeechobee were created to be dominated by the sugar industry.

The lawsuit, filed against the SFWMD for failing since its inception to control the level of P entering the lake, alleged that since 1970 the concentration had more than doubled to 120 ppb, and once it moved south through the heavily fertilized fields of the EAA it increased to 200 ppb.

The optics were not pretty. The United States Government had sued an agency of the State of Florida, and by implication the Corps and the agricultural operations in the EAA. Faced with heavy criticism from state officials, the Justice Department in Washington began to back off, given the political importance of Florida as the Democratic Party increased its hold on both houses of Congress and the presidential election of 1992 loomed. The state, in addition to applying political pressure, was vigorous in its defense against the lawsuit by spending millions of dollars on an array of lawyers.

The Florida Sugar Cane League, seeing handwriting on the wall, petitioned the court to allow it to be an intervenor. Once the motion was granted, sugar added its formidable financial resources to the fray, resources made partly available by the federal price support program that guaranteed a generous annual profit. In the final analysis, the amount money spent on both sides made Lehtinen's suit one of the most expensive in American history.

Senator Lawton Chiles (D-FL), running against Republican Governor Mel Martinez, made the lawsuit the primary issue in his campaign, arguing that the state was spending too much on something that cried out for settlement. When Chiles won, he brought the parties to the table to make a deal at any cost. The judge overseeing the suit approved the agreement in February 1992. But that did not end the litigation. The Florida Sugar Cane League, disliking the terms of the settlement, appealed to the court for a review and thirty independent agricultural entities, heavily backed by sugar, sued the SFWMD for its approval of the plan to clean up the water because it lacked scientific transparency.

With litigation ongoing, tempers were rising. Environmental groups abandoned the façade of civility and became openly hostile to the sugar industry, which responded in kind. The broader and politically connected Florida agricultural community joined in, feeling threatened by the active and energized move toward stricter regulation of the use of nutrients on farm fields.

The suit had another effect. It brought awareness of the problem to the public's attention and created demand for further action made necessary by a developing situation to the immediate south of Everglades National Park, and that was a massive die-off of sea grass in Florida Bay.

COLLAPSE OF FLORIDA BAY

In 1993, the year of the General Accounting Office report on the overall cost of the sugar price support program to American consumers, and payment of large sums to the biggest sugar companies, Florida Bay was in the sixth year of a sea grass collapse followed by a ferocious algal bloom.

Beginning in 1987, the 850 sq. mi. area south of the park and north of Buck Key, with over two dozen inlets and small coves, suffered from hyper salinity as a result of a lack of fresh water. Before the C&SF project to drain the Everglades, fresh water flowed slowly from Lake Okeechobee through the park and into Florida Bay, creating an ecological balance to which the various sea grass populations had adapted. The grasses varied from widgeon and shoal grass near fresh-water outlets, to turtle grass which covered most of the bottom of the outer bay.

Water flowing into the park had already been partially stifled by construction of the Tamiami Trail from Fort Myers through Everglades City and east to Miami. Finished in 1928, it contained a few small culverts but was built at grade across the expanse of south Florida effectively choking off the historic, oozing water flow, but the hydrology changed so slowly that the grasses had time to adapt.

To add to the thoughtlessly constructed barrier of the Trail, Interstate 75, originally a two-lane road known as the Everglades Parkway, was substantially upgraded and finished in 1993, crossing the state to the north of the Trail, then turning east at Naples and ending up in Fort Lauderdale. While the drainage system and wildlife passageways were given some thought, water flow was still choked down into narrow ditches, directed to flow through constricted pipes and then left to its own devices to spread out over the landscape.

Adding to the bad drainage into and out of the ENP, high summer temperatures combined with nutrient releases with little fresh-water flushing caused phytoplankton blooms, upsetting the carbon and nitrogen balance and suffocating the turtle grass which then decomposed releasing sulfide into the water column. As the biomass floated to the surface, it deprived the area of sunlight. Turtle grass could survive in low light but needed enough to photosynthesize carbon dioxide into oxygen. With a lack of oxygenation from the grasses, hypoxia set in and the fish population in Florida Bay began to die. The sulfide was toxic to fish as well, and the sport fishing industry worth nearly $1 billion a year to the economy of the Keys, was in deep trouble. Over 60,000 acres of meadows were affected.

According to one peer-reviewed study:

> "The causes of this mortality are still not well understood, but stresses caused by such factors as high salinity, high temperature, sulfide toxicity, self-shading and hypoxia (caused by biomass accumulation), and infection by the slime mold (*Labrynthula* sp.) are hypothesized to play a role." [130]

As the die-off continued, phytoplankton algal blooms and increased turbidity of the water column spread the devastation. Finally, George Barley, a well-heeled developer from Orlando, his wife Mary, and joined by billionaire investment manager Paul Tudor Jones, had endured enough. They were sport fishermen with a love of the pristine waters of Florida Bay, with its wavy grasses clearly visible in crystal clear water, creating the beauty of an infinite landscape at the southern tip of America.

"It was terrible," said Mary Barley, "we all had pumps going day and night. The water was green and the algae were everywhere. But we couldn't stop it. There was just too much going into the ecosystem." [131]

Gathering together politicians, environmental groups and businesses affected by the die-off of the bay, and calling it *Save our Everglades*, the group raised over 600,000 signatures to put three propositions on the state ballot as a constitutional amendment. The first two propositions would be enabling and the third a 1¢ per pound tax on sugar grown in Florida.

The argument from *Save our Everglades* was that while the settlement of the Lehtinen lawsuit would require farmers in the EAA to pay between $220 and $322 million per year and cost taxpayers in the SFWMD taxing district about $220 million, it seriously underestimated the true cost of cleanup which probably lay in the $700 to $800 million a year range. The proposed 1¢ tax would raise about $875 million a year, provoking a senior vice president of U.S. Sugar to call the situation a case of "mob rule" run by a group of "environmental extremists." [132]

The initiative never made it onto the 1994 ballot. The Florida Supreme Court, in a unanimous decision, ruled that the measure involved more than one subject and was therefore illegal. In unsparingly blunt language, the court went even further alleging that political animus toward sugar motivated the framers of the proposal. "It is as thought the drafters drew up their plan to restore the Everglades, then stepped outside their role as planners, donned judicial robes and made factual findings and determination of liability and damages," wrote Justice Shaw.[133]

The sugar industry was jubilant, as was the spokesman for U.S. Sugar. "If this tax went through we would have been out of business. They want us out of business, so they will continue to do that." [134] Given profit estimates from the GAO report of 1993, the statement from U.S. Sugar was an exaggeration as to the effect of the tax, but prescient as to the future.

EVERGLADES FOREVER ACT

In 1994, the state legislature passed the Everglades Forever Act (EFA). Basing it upon the earlier Marjory Stoneman Douglas Everglades Act, the bill identified two funding sources to be used for restoration: an agricultural privilege tax and a 0.1 mil ad valorem tax on residents within the boundary of the SFWMD. At the time the privilege tax was $24.89 per acre. In essence, the EFA was identical to the earlier act which Douglas asked not bear her name, since she felt it did not go far enough in forcing polluters to pay the cost of restoration.

The bill was filled with nostrums of high-sounding language, heavy on intent but light on execution, which when summarized on the state's website said it would "(e)xecute plans and programs to improve the quantity of water reaching the Everglades" and "(p)ursue comprehensive and innovation solutions to the issues of water quality, water quantity, hydroperiods and invasions of non-native species that affect the Everglades ecosystem." [135] The bill was useful as political cover but useless as an enforceable document to compel restoration.

POLLUTER PAYS

Undaunted by the court setback, *Save Our Everglades* came back again in 1996 with three separate petitions. The first sought to have the SFWMD levy a 1¢ per pound tax on raw sugar grown and processed in Florida for the next 25 years. A second piece asked voters to establish an Everglades Trust Fund to be used for restoration and the third was a separate initiative known as Amendment 5, stating that:

> "Those in the Everglades Agricultural Area who cause water pollution within the Everglades Protection Area or the Everglades Agricultural Area shall be primarily responsible for paying the costs of the abatement of that pollution." [136]

The court decided that each one had a specific, single purpose as stated and could go on the ballot. The second and third passed, but the first—the imposition of a fee on raw sugar—failed.

However, there was a fatal flaw in Amendment 5. There were no provisions, similar to what had been articulated in the Florida Air and Water Pollution Act of 1967, as to how the amendment would be implemented. Issues such as the permissible level of toxins, time limits for compliance, sanctions or fines to be levied for violations, and how guilt should be determined and apportioned among the identified polluters, were all lacking.

On the same ballot in 1996 were three amendments put up by a sugar-backed group called the Tax Cap Committee. That initiative would require a two-thirds vote on any constitutionally imposed fee or tax retroactive back to 1994. Of the $4.6 million raised for the campaign by the

Tax Cap Committee, $3.6 million came from sugar, with U.S. Sugar leading the pack at $2.6 million. It was a brilliant name because the word "tax" was (and still is) anathema to a majority of Florida voters, like waving a red cape in front of a 2,000-pound bull.

Sugar didn't give up there. The industry backed two other groups financially to oppose the *Save our Everglades* amendments. The first, called Alliance of Florida's Sugar-Farmers, produced a set of television ads featuring small growers from the state, giving *bona fides* to the decision back in the 1960s by U.S. Sugar and Alfonso Fanjul, Sr. to support and encourage small growers to form a cooperative to maintain the appearance that Florida sugar wasn't just a duopoly of two major processor/growers.

A second group opposing the amendment, called Citizens to Save Jobs and Stop Unfair Taxes was based in Orlando and received money from U.S. Sugar, the Fanjul privately held Flo-Sun Corporation and the Sugar Cane Growers Cooperative of Florida. According to one press report, sugar backed that group to the tune of $19.4 million.[137] The well-funded opposition to the initiative went for naught as Amendment 5 passed with 68% of the vote.

Once law, Florida Attorney General Robert Butterworth issued an opinion at the request of the SFWMD that:

> "...while the legislature may enact provisions implementing Amendment #5, the amendment itself

establishes an obligation on polluters of the Everglades to pay the costs of abating such pollution *irrespective of legislative action* [italics mine]." [138]

Seeking clarification, Governor Chiles then brought the issue of implementation to the Supreme Court of Florida. Agricultural interests argued that the words "primarily responsible" in the amendment indicated that there should be a sharing of responsibility considering the rapid growth of exurban population in the watershed. This argument was summarily dismissed because the language applied only to the Everglades protection area or the EAA, where there was little development, but the court, to the dismay of environmentalists and delight of the sugar industry, ruled in a 1997 advisory opinion that the amendment was not self-executing and the legislature would have to pass an enabling statute to carefully delineate fulfillment of the terms of the amendment in order for the two agencies responsible for pollution abatement, the SFWMD and Florida Department of Environmental Protection, to enforce the rules as yet unwritten.[139]

The matter slipped through the cracks at the legislature until 2003 when the state Supreme Court entered the picture again. In a review of a Fifth District Court of Appeals 2000 decision on a suit against the SFWMD brought by Mary Barley, whose husband had been killed in a plane crash, the court ruled against the 1996 opinion of Attorney General Robert Butterworth and supported the court's

1997 advisory opinion, driving a stake into the heart of Amendment 5.

By delegating responsibility to the legislature (despite a dissenting opinion that the legislature could not fail to implement the clear will of the people) the matter was pitched headlong into the arcane rules of the Florida House and Senate.

Power in the state legislature lies in the leadership: in the Speaker of the House and the President of the Senate. The Speaker has the power to appoint committee chairs who advance only those bills the Speaker supports and also has the power to keep bills from coming out of a committee to the floor. The leadership is selected four years ahead of time, and assuming the nominees are re-elected, come to power but are beholden to those who selected them from among the forty senators and 120 house members.

The Senate President exercises control through appointment of the Majority Leader, committee chairs and committee members. Although less forceful than some of the rules in the House, committee chairs are generally obedient to will of the person who appointed them to leadership positions.

The sugar lobby reminded legislators that in the 1998 – 1999 election, when Republicans gained control of the governor's office and the legislature, the industry had become one of the largest contributors to the Florida Republican party. The legislature then declared the agricultural privilege tax in effect was the de facto implementing legislation and no further changes were needed. The 2003 court decision stood and the polluter pays amendment was toast.

Les Bon Temps Roll On

Before the 2003 Florida court decision, Congress passed the Farm Security and Rural Investment Act of 2002. A 437-page monster, debate over the bill's provisions for sugar was heated. A General Accounting Office report was highly critical of the program, giving opponents a credible government agency study to challenge the prevailing wisdom that there was "no net cost." Despite brutal opposition, the final version continued the price support program with import limits.

2002 ACT

Strenuous objections were mounted against a background of rising profits for beet and cane companies, but the bill became law in May despite some of the highest price differentials between U.S. and world sugar prices ever seen. In 2001, the U.S. price per pound for raw sugar was 21.1¢; world price was 9¢. In 2002, the domestic price was triple the world price.[140]

The non-recourse loan program was left untouched, and marketing allotments were reinstated if projected imports fell below 1.532 million short tons in an attempt to curtail domestic production to avoid oversupply. The "overall allotment quantity" (OAQ) for domestic production and sale was divided between beet and cane at 54.35% vs 45.65%. The Secretary of Agriculture was given the additional authority to manage inventories in order to balance demand and supply while complying with provisions of NAFTA and the World Trade Organization, especially important since the world was being buried by an oversupply of sugar as reflected in the world price.

Another mechanism for managing inventory was to create the opportunity for producers and processors to buy sugar directly out of the CCC inventory in exchange for a promise to reduce planting areas by an equivalent yield, a boon to the vertically integrated companies doing business in Florida.

Finally, marketing assessments and forfeiture penalty payments levied against processors were ended, and the interest rate on loans issued by the government was reduced even further—showing the power of the sugar lobby in view of the healthy domestic pricing situation while the world price was collapsing.

2003 IN THE FLORIDA HOUSE AND SENATE

In another display of raw naked power by the sugar

industry, the state had agreed in 2001, long after passage of the 1994 Everglades Forever Act, to set a mandated maximum phosphorous level in Lake Okeechobee at 10 parts per billion (ppb) to avoid federal sanctions under the Clean Water Act. By 2003, it was obvious the goal would never be met by the 2016 deadline.

In Florida, if the legislature is unable to move all bills through to the floor of the House and Senate, the clock on the wall is stopped so that the session can continue until all bills are dealt with. In the last moments of the 2003 session, the 2016 deadline was quietly moved back to 2026.

The sugar industry's total political donations for 2002 – 2003 were $673,320 of which $286,831 went to the Republican Party of Florida—controlling both sides of the legislature at the time.[141]

2008 BILL

Back in Washington five years later, major changes were made in the Food, Conservation and Energy Act of 2008. First the OAQ estimate had a floor of 85% for domestic producers. The trigger on allotments was eliminated. If existing allotments for cane were not met, the gap amount would go first to other processors in cane-producing states; the same rule applied to beet production and processors.

No changes were made to trade policies save one: On January 1, 2008, Mexico was allowed to ship unlimited amounts of sugar into the U.S. in accordance with terms of

NAFTA. The Congressional Budget Office (CBO), in scoring the change, warned that if the market was flooded with Mexican sugar it would bring the price down below the loan rate and cause processors to default in large numbers. This brought about the third major change: the bill set out a sugar-for-ethanol program that required the USDA to purchase as much sugar produced by American companies as necessary to maintain a market price above the loan rate level so as to prevent defaults and maintain the "no-cost" provision. No limit was set on the amount that could be purchased.

Corn had been the primary feedstock for ethanol until 2006 when a study from Louisiana State University, in conjunction with multiple federal agencies including the USDA, found that beet and raw cane sugar, as well as molasses, could be converted profitably into ethanol depending upon the price of gasoline. The conversion price for cane was $2.40 per gallon and for beet $2.35 per gallon. Molasses converted would cost $1.27 and corn $1.05 per gallon.

"The estimated ethanol production costs using sugarcane, sugar beets, raw sugar, and refined sugar as a feedstocks are more than twice the production cost of converting corn into ethanol. While it is more profitable to produce ethanol from corn in the United States, the price of ethanol is determined by the price of gasoline and other factors, rather than the cost of producing ethanol from corn. With recent spot market prices for ethanol near $4 per gallon, it is profitable to produce ethanol from sugar cane, sugar beets, raw sugar and refined sugar." [142]

At the urging of producers and processors, the bill also tweaked minimum prices for beet and cane sugar by increasing the loan rates between 4% and 5% by 2012 when the bill would expire. The industry asked for a penny per pound increase but in a compromise, cane would go from 18¢ to 18.75¢ per pound. Beet would go from 22.9¢ to 24.1¢ per pound.

Food and beverage manufacturers opposed the bill on the basis that another round of confectioner price increases to the consumer was inevitable, and President George W. Bush vetoed the bill twice. The Congress overrode both vetoes with the second vote 80–14 in the Senate and an eye-popping 317–109 in the House. But the negotiations between the industry and Congressional representatives, and the two vetoes by President Bush, were indicators of increasing opposition to the price support program and were further illuminated by three factors.

The first was another round of exposés on the treatment of workers in the cane fields. The second was the beginning of a full-court press by business organizations and conservative think tanks concerned that the price support program violated the concepts of free-markets and competition. The third was the environmental movement's insistence that failure of the "polluter pays" amendment was only the first quarter of a long game.

Les Bon Temps
Interrupted

The rights of both domestic and immigrant workers had always been a simmering problem for sugar, resulting in lawsuits and unpleasant publicity for the industry. The H-2 program had been amended in 1986 to add a new category of H-2A to apply to seasonal agricultural workers. It was similar in most respects to the older designation but was cumbersome and expensive, meant to discourage its use over hiring domestic workers.

WORKERS RIGHTS DEFINED

The reason for the need to clearly define workers' rights in the sugar fields went all the way back to the Second World War, to the BWI program, and to the case where U.S. Sugar Corporation was accused of slavery in its Florida business. In the last instance, charges were eventually dropped in 1943 on grounds relating to jury selection, and the case was given little notoriety as the world war was drawing most of the public's attention.

The sugar agro-industry in Florida was sued in 1985 alleging that foreign workers were taking domestic jobs. The industry pushed back saying that the work was hard. "Many of the Americans who try it just don't want to stay," was the comment of George Sorn, a spokesperson for one of the defendants.[143] The case was settled out of court with an agreement to make available jobs well-publicized and advertised.

While there were a number of other smaller actions filed against companies by employees over the ensuing years, a significant action was filed in 1992 against U.S. Sugar, Sugar Cane Growers Cooperative of Florida, Osceola Farms and Okeelanta Corporation by the Farmworkers Justice Fund, brought about in part by Alec Wilkinson's book *Big Sugar: Seasons in the Cane Fields of Florida*.

Wilkinson spent almost a year in South Florida, harassed by law enforcement officials and secretly conducting interviews with workers fearful of retribution for talking with him. He found that the growers, protected by the sugar lobby, import quotas and lax enforcement of the H-2A program, treated their cutters, mainly Jamaican, like slaves. The book graphically described cane planting, burning and harvesting as the most dangerous work in the U.S., with cutters working seven-day weeks, underpaid with a forced savings program and living in barracks buildings made from abandoned railroad boxcars. They were provided the opportunity to buy second-rate goods at company stores and given minimal access to medical care.

The case, *Bygrave v. Okeelanta,* was brought as a class-action on behalf of thousands of workers who felt cheated out of fair compensation. Bernard Bygrave was a Jamaican who had worked for the Fanjul-owned Okeelanta Farms. The suit alleged that he and others had been contracted to receive a wage-equivalent rate of $5.30 per ton for cut cane, but actual payments when calculated out came to only $3.75 using something called the "task rate," an obscure method of calculating the tonnage by rows cut and not by weight. The average worker could cut between seven and ten rows a day, but payment was based upon an arbitrary assessment of the value of each row, not the agreed-on rate.

Each worker, before leaving for the U.S. under the H-2A program was given a contract specifying how payment would be made. To obtain and hold the visa, companies were given a "clearance order" that contained a full description of work to be performed and specifying that an average of eight tons per day throughout the season was the expected rate of harvest for each worker. The ambiguity between the hourly rate at the prevailing minimum wage, the expected productivity of each worker and the "task rate" was wide open for multiple interpretations. And it was all overseen by the Department of Labor, with the responsibility of ensuring that the minimum wage was paid to the workers.

In 1992, the presiding judge issued a summary judgment in the case, awarding workers $51 million in back wages. U.S. Sugar appealed the amount of the award, and three years later, won the appeal.[144] The case was then divided into five separate cases, all jury trials, some of which went on for eight more years.[145]

Eventually, U.S. Sugar settled for $5.1million to avoid extensive legal fees and bad public relations engendered by the complaint. Fulfilling the Mott family's desire to be good citizens, the company invited the media and public into the cane fields to show and explain how sugar was grown and processed, projecting the company as family-friendly and transparent.

The Fanjul companies took a totally different tack, continuing to fight each suit in court and through the appellate process if necessary, while maintaining a strict embargo on media contacts. The family had always been on the "A" list in the Palm Beach and New York social scene but in their business dealings remained obscure and secretive. However, the Fanjul holdings had a checkered record in responding to crisis. In an earlier case, reaction to a massive demonstration of worker discontent showed how they dealt with the situation as reported by the *Palm Beach New Times*:

"On November 22, 1986, a squad of Palm Beach County police in riot helmets with attack dogs had taken on a crew that refused to accept the pay conditions in the Fanjul fields. Some 100 cutters from St. Vincent had balked at the wages offered. As in all labor disputes, a liaison officer was called, but the two sides could not agree on a figure. The workers started to walk the eight miles back to the camp, and the next morning, still with no agreement, 40 of them refused to get on the bus. At that point the Okeelanta personnel manager called in the police. All in all, 384 workers, many of whom had had nothing to do with the argument in the fields, were deported. Cooks in the kitchen, cutters from other parts of the property—all were sent back to the islands. They were not even given time to gather their possessions. T-shirts and boom boxes were strewn all over the ground." [146]

This event became known as the "Dog War" because a number of workers had been bitten by K-9 dogs sent in to break up the riot. The strikers were sent by bus to Miami International Airport and flown back to the Caribbean. The company had no comment when asked about the incident.

CONGRESSIONAL REPORTS ON LABOR

In July 1991, as *Bygrave v. Okeelanta* was being prepared, the House Education and Labor Committee criticized both Florida sugar growers and the U.S. Department of Labor for allowing abusive treatment of cane cutters. In attempting to address the situation with action rather than words, the House committee filed a report naming Okeelanta Corporation as having violated a number of labor standards, mainly by underreporting of actual hours worked and recommending a fine of $2.5 million. The report formed the basis for an attempt to make some minor changes to the H-2A program, including a simplified contract more easily understood, review of the deductions being withheld from workers checks by growers, and a possible re-opening of the files on the 1986 incident at Okeelanta.[147]

As changes were being debated, a spokesman for U.S. Sugar responded that the average cane cutter in its fields earned $7.20 per hour, well above the minimum wage, and all companies cited frankly admitted that they planned to increase the level of mechanized harvest to reduce the use of field workers.

George Wedgworth, founder and long-time chief executive of Sugar Cane Growers Cooperative of Florida said it straight out: "We can't stand the bad press and we're getting out of it." [148] At the time, 83% of the cooperative's harvest was done by machine.

The Fanjuls took the possibility of legislative intervention seriously. They responded by making the case that the committee's charges against Okeelanta were simply a matter of bad bookkeeping and unintentional human error.

A second shoe dropped a year later when the General Accounting Office, the same group that one year later produced a report showing the real cost to consumers of the sugar price support program, took a look at the H-2A program. Consistent with the House committee report of a year earlier, the GAO was highly critical of the Department of Labor for its lack of oversight and lax enforcement of wage and hour standards of guest workers. The greatest concern was the rule that no worker, either domestic or H-2A, could "change employers during the course of the sugar cane harvest." [149]

U.S. Sugar responded immediately by inviting the media to see freshly painted guest worker quarters and recreation halls in their venues, and to offer unfettered access to workers for interviews. The press and TV was generally positive as the company sought to project a paternalistic attitude similar to that of the early days of Nelson Fell's planned town of Fellsmere and Clarence Bitting's vision for a caring physical environment for employees and guest workers.

Beet farmers do not have the same labor problems. They are mostly small and mechanized, gaining scale through cooperatives and grower associations. They are widely dispersed over twelve states and hold great sway with their Congressional delegations. Cane sugar, on the other hand, is more concentrated with a few large companies dominating the market, making them a much more likely target for scandals and lawsuits relating to the guest worker programs and also for the profits they enjoy through the price support program coming under attack from pro-business groups.

CATO

Financial subsidies underlying the farm programs

in the United States had always been looked at as a form of gentle paternalism but tolerated by conservatives and free-market advocates as a part of the landscape insuring a reliable food supply. With sugar included in the protective umbrella of the omnibus farm bills, there was a new sense of security for beet and cane processors and growers but that all began to change in the early 1990s.

Founded in 1974 by the Charles Koch Foundation, the Cato Institute is one of America's leading libertarian think tanks, committed to advocacy and promotion of free market principles. The farm bills over the years were anathema to the organization, and one of the Institute's favorite targets was sugar.

In a report titled *Farm Bill Follies of 1990*, author James Bovard took on the sugar program. With the heading "Sugar Police to the Rescue," he set out the argument:

> "In the 1820s sugar farmers said they needed high tariff protection because they were 'warring with nature' trying to grow sugar (the U.S. climate is comparatively unsuited for sugar production). And for generations Uncle Sam has helped sugar farmers 'fight nature' by forcing consumers to pay unnatural prices for sugar." [150]

In fact, the author was sorely mistaken about the climate being "unsuited" for growing sugar. The Everglades Agricultural Area was as productive as most other parts of the world, but that did not diminish his ardor.

The report continued:

> "Our sugar policy is America's least efficient welfare program. In 1987 sugar farmers had a total income from sugar sales of roughly $300 million. Since the program cost the consumers $3 billion, the policy cost the consumers $10 for each $1 of income sugar farmers received." [151]

Here was the nexus of the argument: the true cost of the sugar price support program was always disguised by the "no net cost" language of the farm bills. There was another layer of cost and that was the cost to the American consumer which Cato and other organizations were determined to calculate and publicize.

In another White Paper five years later, the Institute went after farm programs again. Citing the General Accounting Office's 1993 study on sugar, Cato framed it as an "egregious taxpayer subsidy" when:

> ". . . (a)n estimated 40 percent of the $1.4 billion sugar price support program benefits the largest 1 percent of sugar farms. The 33 largest sugar plantations each receive more than $1 million." [152]

GAO 2000

Adding to the pressure to look hard at the true cost of the sugar program, the General Accounting Office followed up its 1993 study with a second report at the request of Senator Diane Feinstein (D-CA) and Representatives George Miller (D-CA) and Dan Miller (R-FL), a conservative member of Congress who believed the support program should be either modified or abolished.

In a letter to the elected officials, the GAO reaffirmed the $1.4 billion cost set out in the 1993 study, noting that it had recommended "... that the Congress gradually lower the loan rate for sugar and direct USDA to adjust import quotas accordingly to achieve a lower U.S. market price. The 1996 Farm Act did not revise the sugar program along the lines we had recommended." [153]

Estimates of the cost to consumers, based upon world prices, amounted to $1.5 billion in 1996 and $1.9 billion in 1998, with the difference due to a decline in the world price while the domestic price remained about the same. If the program was eliminated, the GAO estimated the net advantage would be $700 million in 1996 and $900 million in 1998 taking into account an offset of net losses and economic efficiencies as farmers adjusted their crop mix.

The price of HFCS, according to the new study, would be unaffected. In the 1993 study, it was a few pennies per pound cheaper than beet or cane. In the intervening seven years, it had dropped dramatically due to production efficiencies and, if the sugar program was scrapped, the study assumed corn sugar would not have to reduce prices any further to remain competitive with foreign sugar.

The Sugar Alliance, consisting of a large group of producers, processors and some refiners (those tightly integrated into producer/processor operations), disputed the report's conclusions based upon absence of information about the cost of production in other countries. The model was criticized for its assumptions that the world price would remain unchanged if the U.S. phased out price supports. It also challenged the assumption that candy makers and other manufacturers would pass along 100% of the price break to consumers. But the main argument was that any modification to the program would result in the loss of good American jobs.

The jobs argument would become more significant, and bite into the Sugar Alliance argument over time, as candy companies moved operations out of the U.S. to find cheaper labor and raw sugar. An opening repudiation of this came later from the president of the National Confectioners Association as reported in a 2012 blog from the American Enterprise Institute:

> "The [US sugar] program creates a competitive advantage for foreign confectioners who pay a significantly lower world price for sugar and import their products into the US market. The tight market generated by these

policies threatens the overall supply, jeopardizing smaller US companies and putting jobs at risk. Over the last 10 years the sugar program has eliminated more than 14,000 confectionery jobs and more than 75,000 food manufacturing jobs." [154]

CAFTA-DR

In 2004, the United States opened negotiations for a multilateral trade agreement with a group of Central American countries in the interest of promoting hemispheric stability through economic cooperation. Sugar imports were a critical part of the discussion. However, the Dominican Republic, a large sugar producer, was not included in the first round, but entered within months after discussions began—for a very good reason.

In 1984, the Fanjul family had made a deal to buy assets of the Gulf & Western Company, one of the first conglomerates built by Charles Bludhorn during an era when American companies were acquiring a wide variety of assets in different businesses. The Fanjul Flo-Sun Land Holdings and other corporations under the family's control acquired 240,000 acres of sugar-growing land, a mill and a desirable resort called *Casa de Campo* in the Dominican Republic as part of the deal. Included were 90,000 acres of sugar farms in Florida, a processing facility and a refinery. The price was never openly divulged, but according to the *New York Times* it was in the neighborhood of $200 million.[155]

The Fanjul interests did not want to be left out of the pending CAFTA agreement because it provided a perfect pipeline for export from its Dominican company to the United States in the first tranche of low-tariff imports. Its company, Central Romana, was the island's largest producer and processor generating over half the country's raw sugar, and every ton imported into the U.S. would be bought at the pegged domestic price.

Year	World Price ¢	New York Price (duty paid)
2002	6.4	20.6
2003	7.3	21.8
2004	6.5	20.5
2005	9.1	20.9
2006	14.8	22.6
2007	10.3	20.9
2009	11.7	22.1
2010	21.0	34.2 [156]

The above chart shows that in the years prior to signing of the CAFTA-DR agreement, the domestic price was running as high as three times the world price. In addition, the in-quota tariff was set at 0.625¢ per pound for raw sugar. The out-of-quota tariff was set at 16.21¢ for refined sugar, a case of legislated protectionism and favoritism to those countries lucky enough to get in under the in-quota limit.

Central Romana bought sugar from independent farmers and relied also upon the *colonos* system of linked growers. It cut some of its fields using manual labor in order to maintain employment in the country, but manual cutting in the Dominican was performed for the most part by Haitians. Fleeing across the island for higher wages, working conditions were oppressive but the CAFTA-DR agreement included a section committing all parties to ensure that fair labor standards would be met in exchange for preferential import allotments at the in-quota tariff rate.

With a large part of its annual harvest going to the U.S., the Fanjul operations were extremely profitable and easily able to tolerate higher costs of harvest "on the knife" as the price for economic stability within the Dominican Republic.

2012 FARM BILL

To increase pressure to either alter or eliminate the price support program, proponents adopted a strength in numbers strategy with the Congress. The 2008 bill was to be reviewed and renewed in 2012, and the Coalition for Sugar Reform (CSR), a broad-based group of confectioners, began the debate by running a slick public relations campaign called "Unwrap the Facts."

It was a bit curious that confectioners would lead the charge against the support program. They were normally in the same corner with the sugar agro-industry when it came to health issues, and in 2010 based on a 2,000 calorie diet, about 16% of calories consumed by the average American came from added sugar.

A Senate Committee bill to reauthorize the 2008 program and keep it intact until 2017 was reported out to the floor, but the Coalition's allies were ready. They filed eight bills in the House to

> ". . . repeal all statutory authorities pertaining to sugar marketing, quotas and allotments, payments made to processors to store sugar forfeited to the U.S. Department of Agriculture (USDA), storage facility loans, and the feedstock flexibility program for bioenergy producers (i.e. the sugar-to-ethanol) program." [157]

As sugar became more and more vertically integrated, growers, processors and refiners were more united by common interests in maintaining the program on as "as-is" basis.

Recognizing this, the Coalition changed strategy and attempted to revise but not completely revoke sugar policy by retaining the basic elements of the program, with the exception of the sugar-to-ethanol feedstock option, by a modification to the quotas and allotments, and by giving the Secretary more flexibility in managing the program in areas that had been previously restricted in the 2008 bill. With the Congress at a stalemate, it became clear that no new bill would pass, and the 2008 bill stayed as the governing authority for the sugar program. Changes would have to wait until the next Congress was seated in 2014.

In the following years, the domestic price bubble burst and prices dropped below the loan forfeiture level for cane sugar, requiring the USDA to purchase $141 million in 2013 and $118 million in 2014. Beet sugar remained barely above the loan rate. By July 2014, the price had moved up to a more comfortable 24¢ per pound for cane, where it would stay for the next two years.

Year	World Price ¢	New York Price (duty paid)
2011	28.4	38.5
2012	22.9	32.5
2013	18.0	21.0
2014	16.8	23.1
2015	13.4	24.7 [158]

UPPING THE ANTE

Money spent to hire lobbyists and campaign contributions was moving up, too. In 1990, candidates received a little over $2 million from beet and cane sugar companies. By 2010 that number had increased to about $4.7 million, with Democrats receiving the lion's share as they controlled the Congress and the White House. Lobbying expenses of about $2.7 million in 1990 grew to $7.5 million in 2010.

The Fanjul companies felt particularly vulnerable, their image still burdened by revelations of the General Accounting Office over the situation in the Dominican Republic. They were accelerating political donations as they were expanding by finishing the purchase of the Tate & Lyle plc European operations through one of their subsidiaries, American Sugar Refining, jointly owned by Florida Crystals Corporation and Sugar Cane Growers Cooperative of Florida. The acquisition ended a three-step process begun in 2001 with purchase of Domino Sugar and its three refineries, followed in 2007 by acquiring the Canadian operations of Tate & Lyle with another refinery, and concluding in 2010.

After closing the deal in 2010, ASR had ten refineries and five processing mills with an annual output of six million tons of refined sugar throughout the world. The largest plant was in Louisiana and produced nearly one million tons of refined sugar. In Florida's EAA, the company had 187,000 acres and the Co-op another 65,000 acres. When adding in the acreage owned by Central Romana in the Dominican Republic, the vertically integrated Fanjul-controlled businesses had become the most powerful privately-owned sugar producer and marketer in the Free World. They had a sweet deal with the price support program and CAFTA-DR in-quota imports into the U.S. and they intended to keep it. To do that required a host of lobbyists and enough legislators in Congress to see things their way, with help from the beet growers in twelve states, cane farmers and processors in Louisiana, U.S. Sugar Corporation in Florida, and the powerful American Farm Bureau Federation looking out for its members.

By 2012, total sugar company contributions to 140 Democrats and to 130 Republicans in the House and Senate totaled $5.5 million with the total dollars weighted almost 2–1 for Democrats. Flo-Sun, a Fanjul company, contributed over $1 million to the effort, up from $800,000 in 2010.

AHA MOMENT

With the cacophony of opposition to the sugar program rising, and to the apparent horror of the other Florida companies, U.S. Sugar announced on June 24, 2008 that it would sell 187,000 acres of land in the EAA to connect water flow from Lake Okeechobee to Florida Bay and Everglades National Park once again. The price would be $1.37 billion.

Immediately thereafter, the 2009 recession hit Florida hard. Tax receipts from all sources dried up and the state faced deficit financing. The SFWMD board, despite strenuous and vocal objections from the Fanjul-owned Florida Crystals, made an offer to buy 73,000 acres of the land, with an option to add another 56,000 acres, expiring in 2015, when and if funds became available.

In the end, the state purchased only 27,000 acres. Sugar prices, which had made operations only marginally profitable from 2006 to 2010, rose to record levels in 2011 and 2012, causing U.S. Sugar to rethink its original offer after making record profits.

The company, after reversing course, then convinced Governor Rick Scott to ignore the option. Scott had been the beneficiary of sugar's largesse in campaign contributions, and after a secretive 2013 trip to King Ranch in Texas, he appointed Mitchel Hutchcraft, a King Ranch executive to the SFWMD board which later summarily rejected the 2015 option to buy the 56,000 acres.

King Ranch is primarily a citrus grower in Florida but owns 12,000 acres near Belle Glade on which it grows sugarcane. Since 2007, after Hutchcraft joined the company, political contributions to the Republican Party, in control of the state since 1999, totaled $41,150. The Democratic Party, during that same period, received $500. [159]

2013

During the 2013 session of Congress, Senator Richard Lugar (R-IN) introduced a bill to flat shut down the sugar program. It was backed by CSR with members including the U.S. Chamber of Commerce, Club for Growth, Kraft Foods, National Association of Manufacturers, American Beverage Association, and Americans for Tax Reform and the Everglades Trust.

The bill went down in defeat. Among the senators voting against it were Senator Marco Rubio (R-FL) who had been given a fundraiser in New York City by Alfonso and Pepe Fanjul raising $100,000. Senator Bill Nelson (D-FL) was also a "no vote" having received $42,000 from the sugar industry.

The argument made by CSR was that confectionary jobs were fleeing overseas, or raising prices, noting that Jelly Belly, producer of 20% of the jelly beans sold in the U.S., owned by one family for six generations and President Regan's favorite candy sitting in a jar on the Resolute Desk, was forced into moving operations out of the country after raising prices due to the high cost of domestic sugar. [160]

THE FIRST BEGHIN AND ELOBEID STUDY

While the GAO and Economic Research Service of the USDA produced studies on a regular basis to inform Congress on the state of agriculture when a farm bill was due for renewal, private studies on the sugar program were usually performed on behalf of clients like the sugar industry or its opponents. This was the case when an economic forensic was done in 2013 by two professors at Iowa State University on the economic cost of the sugar program. The results were summarized as follows:

"We analyze the various welfare costs, transfers, trade, and employment consequences of the current U.S. sugar program for U.S. consumers, other sugar users, sugar refiners, cane and beet growing and processing industries, other associated agricultural sectors, and world markets. The removal of the sugar program would increase U.S. consumers' welfare by $2.9 to $3.5 billion each year and generate a modest job creation of 17,000 to 20,000 new jobs in food manufacturing and related industries. Imports of sugar containing products would fall dramatically, especially confectioneries substituting for domestic inputs under the sugar program. Sugar imports would rise substantially to 5 to 6 million short tons raw sugar equivalent. World price increases would be minor, equivalent to about 1 cent per pound." [161]

The study was commissioned by the Sweetener Users Association, a trade group, and was heavily disputed by the sugar industry. But it set the stage for the debate on the next farm bill.

2014 FARM BILL

In the 2014 elections, Republicans gained control of the House while extending the party's majority in the Senate. The sugar program had some support across the aisle to continue with price support and sugar-to-ethanol for another five years, but the outcome was uncertain. Sugar's campaign contributions to candidates flipped only a little as the amount stayed around $5.6 million, with the dollars about evenly divided between the two parties.

Debate on the floor of both chambers was heated. Beet and cane growers and processors wanted no changes. Opponents like CSR put forth identical bills in the House and Senate titled as the Sugar Reform Act, arguing that the Congressional Budget Office scoring showed a savings to the government of $82 million over the next decade by passing the reform bill, citing the fact that in late 2013 and 2014, the government had purchased $259 million of collateralized sugar as the market price failed to stay above the loan rate.

On the other side of the equation, with sugar now embedded in every farm bill, the powerful American Farm Bureau Federation and National Farmers Union weighed in to support sugar's position, as did a number of countries with favored in-quota import allotments—including the Dominican Republic.

The bill finally passed as the Agricultural Act of 2014 retaining all of the 2008 provisions including the mandatory OAQ at 85% of projected consumption reserved for domestic processors and producers. The in-quota tariff remained at 0.625¢ and the out of quota at a prohibitive 16.21¢. Imports from Mexico, having caused the market to collapse in late 2012 and early 2013, were restricted as to both quantity and price.

THE SECOND BEGHIN AND ELOBEID STUDY

In 2017, a second forensic was done for the American Enterprise Institute, a conservative think tank. Authors Beghin (having moved to North Carolina State University) and Elobeid (remaining at Iowa State University) reactivated their economic model using later data from 2016. The introduction was an indictment of the program at a new level:

> "Domestic markets are distorted, sugar users are effectively taxed by the program, and sugar producers are subsidized by it. The welfare transfer to sugar growers and processors is quite large in the aggregate, hovering around $1.2 billion. Losses to households are diffused, about $10 per person per year but large for the population as a whole, in the range of $2.4–$4 billion. Net welfare losses are smaller and are in the order of $0.5–$1 billion. *Gains to producers are concentrated in a few hands, especially in the cane sugar industry* [Italics mine]. Labor effects from lost activity in food industries are between 17,000 and 20,000 jobs annually. The sugar program distorts trade in sugar-intensive imports, which increase to abate the high cost of sugar. The North Atlantic Free Trade Agreement has created additional entanglements as US sugar interests have recently pushed the US government to impose trade management practices on sugar imports from Mexico." [162]

The study calculated job losses in the sugar-producing and processing segments of the American economy as against jobs lost in sugar-using businesses in an attempt to put numbers to the "no-net-cost" provisions included in all farm bills since 1977. There was another message from the analysis: most of the government money was flowing to a few unnamed companies in Florida, and there were only two that would definitely qualify.

Both studies by Beghin and Elobeid had gravity. They were well-sourced and while the logic in their models was based upon a series of assumptions about jobs and prices, the studies provided fodder for opponents of the sugar program to take to Congressional staffers in support of their message. And, as with the 2013 paper, the second Beghin and Elobeid report was released, just before debate in Congress began on the 2018 farm bill.

MEXICO

If there was any hope that the administration of President Donald Trump, with its "America First" agenda, would alter the price support program, it was quickly dashed by a new trade pact with Mexico.

Following the 2012 and 2013 dumping of Mexican sugar into the U.S. market, a bilateral trade agreement limited the import levels of both raw and refined sugar and set minimum prices for both. The 2017 agreement was an extension of the general terms of NAFTA with slight modifications to import limits and price.

The American Sugar Alliance said that the deal would stabilize prices for farmers and refiners, framing it as a "law enforcement issue" after excess world supply had shut down Hawaii's production in December 2016.[163]

On the other side, the president of the Sweetener Users Association, Rick Pasco, was incensed by the short-sightedness of the Trump administration which had made jobs a central part of its agenda. "From a jobs perspective, there are 600,000 people working in the sugar-using industry. The sugar processing sector only employs 18,000 people." [164]

Another line of argument, a familiar refrain, was the cost of the sugar program to the American consumer. According to Professor Robert Kudrle of the University of Minnesota, the tab was around $10 to $11 "for every man, woman and child in the U.S." [165] This was vigorously opposed by the sugar association which responded that there was no guarantee that confectioners and other sugar users would lower retail prices if the cost of sugar was allowed to settle at the world price.

Any change to sugar policy would have to wait. The year 2017 saw the beginning of a sixteen-month long red tide and cyanobacteria outbreak that would plague southwest and east coast Florida estuaries. It was caused by nutrient-laden water coming down the St. Lucie and Caloosahatchee Rivers, forcing a hard look at the source of the problem.

Power Politics

By 2018, environmental issues in Florida had been building for over thirty years. The data out of Lake Okeechobee was gloomy. The 730 sq. mi. water body had been inundated with nitrogen and phosphorous from the 700,000 acres of farm fields, 450,000 of it from cane sugar controlled by two giant, industrial, agricultural operations: U.S. Sugar and the Fanjul-owned companies. While dairy farmers north of the lake had been struggling to keep all animal waste within farm boundaries, cattle ranching had fewer restrictions and allowed their herds to freely pollute the groundwater system with the result that the level of existing phosphorous rose from 30 parts per billion (ppb) to 120 ppb in the 1990s. In addition, there was hardened bottom muck, a layer estimated to comprise over 36 thousand metric tons of phosphorous at the benthic level in the lake.

Lake Okeechobee was declared an impaired water body in 1998, requiring calculation of a total maximum daily load (TMDL) per Sec. 303(d) of the Clean Water Act

(CWA). A TMDL under the CWA is the starting point to clean up a river or a lake by establishing a maximum level of pollutants allowed to enter the water body. The load to be achieved by 2015, as set forth by Florida, was 105 metric tons from the watershed and 35 metric tons from atmospheric deposition. In 2018, the input load to the lake was 1,046 tons—seven times the maximum. In the same year, nitrogen input was 7,512 metric tons, but there was, and still is, no TMDL for nitrogen which is becoming as much of a problem as phosphorous worldwide and in Florida.[166]

To add to the industry's burdens, medical evidence was beginning to show that increased consumption of sugar, primarily fructose, was associated with heart disease. In a 2015 study, researchers concluded:

"Consuming beverages containing 10%, 17.5%, or 25%... from HFCS produced dose-dependent increases in circulating lipid/lipoprotein risk factors for CVD and uric acid within 2 wk. *These results provide mechanistic support for the epidemiologic evidence that the risk of cardiovascular mortality is positively associated with consumption of increasing amounts of added sugars* [italics mine]." [167]

The *Wall Street Journal*, staunch defender of free market capitalism, opined in a 2016 editorial:

> "Americans pay nearly twice as much per pound as foreigners do for sugar, thanks to U.S. import restrictions and subsidies. We've tilted at this corporate welfare for decades, but new political forces are aligning to take another run. The absurdity of the federal sugar program is legendary." [168]

2018 FARM BILL

Spurred on by accumulating evidence as to the environmental and health problems, reform organizations went at it hard in 2018, lobbying the president's agricultural adviser and Commerce Secretary Wilbur Ross to get the Trump administration to oppose price support for sugar. The farm bill was in trouble from the beginning. It suffered a setback in the House in May when Democrats, fighting job training and work provisions for food stamp recipients and Freedom Caucus Republicans wanting immigration reform, cobbled together a 213 – 198 vote against the bill.

Sensing an opening, opponents brought to the floor an amendment to change the terms of the sugar price supports. It was an attempt to separate sugar from the larger and grander farm bill, but went down in defeat 278 – 137, illustrating again the power of the sugar lobby. The main argument against changes was protectionist, that domestic producers and processors were always disadvantaged by foreign governments subsidizing their own sugar companies. The opposition's arguments once again fell flat and Congress quickly passed the Agricultural Improvement Act of 2018 while increasing the loan rate to 19.75¢ for cane processors and 25.38¢ for beet processors.

For one possible explanation of how the sugar industry has been so successful in protecting its guaranteed profit, a further look at political expenditures provides some obvious clues.

MOTHER'S MILK OF POLITICS

As the political, medical and environmental opposition to sugar price supports, market allotments and import controls grew, Florida's sugar companies reacted by increasing their political contributions. The chart below shows total monies paid to candidates and campaigns from political action committees, individuals affiliated with three companies, and a trade association. In order, they are the Fanjul holdings including Florida Crystals, the United States Sugar Corporation, the Sugar Cane Growers Cooperative of Florida, and the Florida Sugar Cane League (a trade association listed as a non-profit on its web site comprised mainly of the first three companies listed below) as expressed in thousands.[169]

Company	2014	2016	2018	2019-2020
Fanjul	$824	$2,607	$1,124	$1,577
U.S. Sugar	$243	$1,201	$269	$365
Co-op	$106	$147	$64	$128
League	$218	$258	$357	$353

Giving to candidates and campaign committees wasn't enough because money in politics was being shoveled into the system by confectioners, candy companies and other opponents. The next best avenue for gaining purchase in the Congress and in Tallahassee was to buy a bevy of lobbyists. This was more the norm as the numbers below show (as expressed in thousands):

Company	2014	2016	2018	2019-2020
Fanjul	$1,190	$1,140	$1,310	$1,010
U.S. Sugar	$200	$450	$1,250	$1,050
League	$1,120	$1,360	$1,360	$1,360
Co-op			$90	$120

The cooperative had dropped out of the trade association in 2014 but rejoined in April 2018 when it resumed giving $30,000 per quarter to lobbying efforts.[170]

TALLAHASSEE

Washington was responsible for passing farm bills, but sugar interests were equally interested in keeping the Florida state legislature and executive branch in a cooperative mood by hiring dozens of lobbyists. The chart below refers to full year lobbying expenses for 2019 (as expressed in thousands):

Company	Legislature	Executive
Fanjul	$875	$110 – $380
U.S. Sugar	$880	$190 – $540
League	$ 20	
Co-op	$ 60	

The Florida state website, curiously, does not report an exact amount for executive lobbying. For example, the reported expense for U.S. Sugar was a range on the website between $190,024 and $539,965.[171]

In addition to hiring lobbyists, the Fanjul family and executives from U.S. Sugar maintained close personal contact with politicians capable of influencing choices made in both the executive and legislative branches of federal and state government. Hunting trips to the King Ranch in Texas and golf at Clewiston were favorite destinations for legislators, but the prize was a trip to the Dominican Republic.

The Fanjul brothers entertained three presidents over the years at their *Casa de Campo* resort in the Dominican, and in one oft-repeated incident on President's Day in 1996, President Bill Clinton was interrupted by a phone call during an *entre nous* with a young intern named Monica Lewinsky. In her deposition with Special Counsel Kenneth Starr she was asked about the caller and replied that it was "... something like Fanuli." [172]

The back story was that Vice President Al Gore, a few hours before the call from Alfonso Fanjul, had announced support for a 1¢ per pound tax on sugar processers to help pay for a $1.5 billion clean-up of the Everglades and the House was debating a measure to gradually phase out the price support program, which eventually failed. The phone call took twenty minutes. To be able to reach a president at a moment like that was a demonstration of real power.

A Burning Issue

To add to the woes created by sugar reform groups and health advocates, the Florida sugar industry found itself as defendants in a 2019 class action suit filed by residents of Palm Beach County. The suit alleged that burning off sugar fields before harvest had compromised the health of citizens who inhaled the smoke.[173]

BLACK SNOW

There are two ways to harvest sugar: green and burnt. To harvest green, machines come into the fields and simply cut the cane. With sucrose in the lower part of the stalk, and the middle of the stalk useful as *bagasse*, the leafy over story is left to fall on the soil where it can either remain or be raked off.

The result of green cutting is that around 30% of the plant's biomass is left on the ground. Research has shown that if green harvesting occurs early it stifles *ratoon* growth and biomass, the ground could suffer from lower temperatures during a frost (extremely rare south and east of Lake Okeechobee), and may lead to more pests reproducing under the cane trash.

Burnt harvest occurs from October to May, after a controlled blaze burns off the "over story," leaving only stalks for the machines to cut. Burnt cutting has been preferred because it increases the sucrose yield in the stalk and makes the plants easier and cheaper to harvest, but fields with burnt harvest require more irrigation and the cane must be processed within twenty-four hours because the sucrose deteriorates more quickly.

The suit alleged that burning in the south Florida sugar fields took place only when the winds were right. A wind blowing smoke to the east might end up in wealthy towns like Palm Beach or Boca Raton, but when blowing to the west the smoke would end up in poorer communities like Belle Glade and Pahokee, home to many minorities and guest workers. It was called the Hazard Zone. According to the plaintiffs, medical statistics from the area defined in the suit showed asthma hospitalizations running five times the average as opposed to all other areas in Palm Beach County.

The class action was filed against ten different sugar companies, but U.S. Sugar decided to meet the issue head-on. In a departure from its normal low-key way of dealing with controversy, it launched a massive public relations campaign based upon a white paper titled *State of Our Air Report* in October 2020.

U.S. Sugar took measurements of particulate matter at

2.5 microns or greater from the FDEP two stations in Belle Glade and West Palm Beach and concluded that there was no difference between air quality during the harvest season and after the harvest was complete.[174] It went on to note that the particulate matter at the West Palm Beach station was higher than at Belle Glade, but that the instruments used "to report the AQI are not federally approved instruments, but are suited to the climate in Florida and are subjected to the same quality assurance and quality control requirements as those used for designations." [175]

Attorneys for the aggrieved residents seized upon that last point and produced their own data. Using a model constructed by the EPA measuring a number of different pollutants, the plaintiff's attorneys asserted after burning over 264,000 acres of cane plants that some of the airborne smoke contained carcinogenic particles which eventually were either inhaled or settled like black snow on residents' property.[176]

According to the EPA:

> "Particulate matter contains microscopic solids or liquid droplets that are so small that they can be inhaled and cause serious health problems. Some particles less than 10 micrometers in diameter can get deep into your lungs and some may even get into your bloodstream. Of these, particles less than 2.5 micrometers in diameter, also known as fine particles or PM2.5, pose the greatest risk to health." [177]

COVID-19

The lawsuit was amended once the COVID-19 crisis hit. One of the byproducts of burning is particulate matter or PM2.5. A Harvard University study cited in the complaint stated that "...an increase of just one microgram of particulate matter pollution (or PM2.5) per cubic meter of air (or $\mu g/m^3$) is associated with and 8% increase in the COVID-19 death rate." [178]

Since the virus affected the lungs, smoke inhalation would aggravate the problem, but the sugar industry continued to burn, despite recommendations from the Centers for Disease Control to either reduce or cease open burning during the crisis.

SCIENCE GREEN VS BURNT

Since sugar is the largest crop grown worldwide, the issue of how to harvest and sustain the most practical level of soil fertility and crop management is important. There have been a number of studies done on Florida cane, and most have been somewhat inconclusive. One study contrasting the effects on both muck and sand found that dealing with post-harvest trash from muck plants was the main reason the practice was not widely adopted.[179]

As to the productivity of either method, another study was based on:

"...sugarcane harvest management effects were

studied on plant cane and two ratoon crops grown on organic Histosols in Florida and plant cane and three ratoon crops grown on clay loam soils in Costa Rica. The harvest systems included burnt cane harvest (Burnt), green cane harvest (Green), and green cane harvest with residue management," concluded that ". . . keeping harvest residue on soil surface after green cane harvest may have neutral effects on sugarcane yields in Florida and Costa Rica." [180]

Residue in the fields from green harvest could be either raked or mulched, but the Sugar Cane Growers Cooperative of Florida dismissed the idea saying it was simply impractical.

Another study done in Ecuador and published in 2008 contained an interesting point about the green vs burnt controversy:

"After considering the impact of all the parameters that were monitored, economic analysis currently favours burned-cane harvest. Conversely, we believe that if better trash-extraction was achieved and if the nutrient recycling of the trash blanket was quantified, the balance would tip in favour of green harvest." [181]

The two words "economic analysis" may explain why Florida sugar companies choose to burn their fields before harvest. Trash extraction or mulching would add to the cost and adding to the cost would reduce the profit.

Brazil, the largest sugar grower in the world, is gradually converting from burnt to green. The country has mandated that all sugar harvesting will be green by the year 2031.

The science of green vs burnt is still unsettled in this country because of the variables involved in soil type and moisture, methods of dealing with cane trash, and weather. But one thing was clear from the allegations in the lawsuit: the possibility that some 40,000 people living in three zip codes in Palm Beach County were suffering health issues and property deterioration in an area blanketed by smoke from cane fields burning from October to May as a result of "economic analysis."

Summing Up

Looking back over the history of sugar in Florida, certain conclusions are obvious and others less so. The economic impact of sugar in the state is relatively small when compared to development and tourism, but the environmental impact has been broad and far-reaching.

SUGAR IN AMERICA

Sugar accounts for less than 1% of the cash receipts received by American farmers for all agricultural crops but is outsized by its influence in the economy. On a national scale, it was used as an instrument of foreign policy beginning in the Gilded Age with Cuba and the Philippines and ending with the 1959 Castro revolution. It has been the subject of a series of bilateral trade agreements with Mexico and used to prop up unstable Caribbean nations where the fear of rebellion lies just beneath the surface.

The use of sugar as a policy instrument was helpful to the industry because it gave purchase to the protectionist argument; that national security depended upon a steady and reliable supply of sugar. This was reinforced in two world wars where sugar was a critical element in the manufacture of munitions, and where sources in both Europe and Asia dried up as a result of the raging conflicts.

The same argument brought the question of foreign subsidies into the equation where protectionism of sugar production, processing and refining in other countries rendered the U.S. at a disadvantage in the world market. The world price was actually based on a small amount of product available for sale, less than 15% of world production coming out of host countries, and that normally happened when oversupply existed to drive the price down.

Foreign competition wasn't the only concern. Public health has been negatively impacted by overconsumption of sugar. In the 1970s, beverage makers began to introduce liquid sweetener from corn syrup further processed to convert some of its glucose into fructose. As it gained popularity, it took market share away from refined sugar, and was the main culprit in a burgeoning epidemic of obesity and type 2 diabetes. Medical researchers were aware that fat and excess calories all contributed to multiple health problems but began to focus on sugar as another contributor to coronary artery disease. HFCS consumption peaked in 1999 but it remained as a low-cost alternative, mainly in liquid form, to compete with refined sugar for market share.

The American sugar industry was never completely united in its objectives. Louisiana, and later Texas, competed with Florida for marketing allotments, and the sugarcane interests were always pushing against beet quotas. However, when it came time to pass a farm bill, all differences were set aside in order to keep a good thing going.

Opposition built over the years. Free market advocates increased their objections to the price support program using respected economists to argue that the net effect on the American economy, in both total jobs lost and the out-of-pocket cost to consumers, was unacceptable in a capitalist country. Sugar users, candy makers and confectioners, began to organize in the 1980s to be able to press a case in Congress for lower prices through more imports, but were beaten back every time a farm bill came up for consideration. The main weapon was money flowing into the pockets of lobbyists, elected representatives and the two major political parties.

SUGAR IN FLORIDA

Florida producers and processors faced a problem unique to the state: excess phosphorous and nitrogen loading of Lake Okeechobee leading to eutrophication of the lake and degradation of water quality flowing south into Everglades National Park and Florida Bay. Louisiana did not have the problem since nutrient runoff from cane fields washed down the Mississippi River along with waste from farms as far north as Minnesota and toxins from chemical factories lining the riverbank. All these contributed to the infamous hypoxic Dead Zone covering up to 8,000 sq. mi. in the Gulf of Mexico. Polluters in the Mississippi River drainage were hard to identify—not so in Florida.

Relentless pressure from environmentalists was countered at the legislature where, time after time, lawmakers either sat on bills as in the case of the "polluter pays" constitutional amendment, or simply kicked the can down the road. The shame was that environmental problems were, and still are, within a single watershed, controlled by jurisdiction of a single entity, the SFWMD.

In Florida, workers' issues kept poking up beginning with the suit against U.S. Sugar for "white slavery" and continuing with Department of Labor reports of abuses of migrant and H-2A field hands. The two largest companies treated complaints differently. U.S. Sugar, coming from a background of paternalism promoted by Clarence Bitting and the Mott family, attempted to settle matters by initiating a public engagement strategy promoting the company as a family business. The intensely private Fanjul companies always dug in, fighting every step of the way against litigation, building up legal fees in an attempt to exhaust the plaintiffs. For both companies, and the co-op, there was an easy way out of the labor problems—mechanization of the harvest—and fewer men "on the knife."

While the early history of Florida sugar included social experiments like the New Smyrna colony and Nelson Fell's planned community as an integral part of their business ventures, sugar inexorably moved toward vertical integration of farming, processing and refining to generate economies of scale with resulting savings and fattening of the bottom line. Support of co-ops, by spreading the work out and providing processing capacity to take harvested crops from smaller independent farmers, attempted to dispel the charge that Florida sugar was a duopoly.

In the final analysis, the Florida sugar industry had the benefit of soil, climate and a favorable political pathway smoothed by copious campaign contributions and guided by legions of lobbyists. As it grew in acreage, it also grew in influence. It enjoyed minimization of risk to the point where profits were guaranteed by a government mandated floor, with virtually no ceiling. It was run, since World War II, by determined entrepreneurs having learned from the mistakes of the past, and by Cuban expatriates bringing their agricultural expertise and hard-nosed business sense to the muck of the once pristine Everglades.

U.S. Sugar has grown from 36,000 to 180,000 acres today in the EAA and the Fanjul companies from 4,000 to over 120,000. The question is: why would they expand, if it was a marginal business. Answer: they wouldn't. The price support program has been highly profitable for the Florida sugar industry at the expense of the American consumer and jobs lost in the confectioner and candy enterprises.

Even more remarkable is how the Congress, every five years, establishes a price for raw sugar, with absolutely no certain knowledge of the cost structure of the industry. For almost every other government program, transparency is required but for some reason this has never applied to sugar.

Every year in Tallahassee, and with every renewal of the farm bill in Congress, come new challenges to Florida's sugar barons, from fair labor standards advocates, environmentalists, sugar users, health advocates and Florida citizens affected by smoke from burning cane fields. Those challenges have always been rebuffed after being met by money from sugar—which in the final analysis is really money that comes from us.

INDEX

ENDNOTES

1 Artschwager, E. and E. W. Brandes, *Sugar Cane Origin, classification and description of representative clones.* U.S. Department of Agriculture Handbook 122, Washington D.C. 1958.

2 Sandiford, Keith. *Theorizing a Colonial Caribbean-Atlantic Imaginary: Sugar and Obeah.* Routledge Press, London, 2015. p. 37.

3 Sandhu, H., Singh, M.P., Gilbert, R., and Odero, D.C. *Sugarcane Botany: A Brief View.* SS-AG-234. UF/IFAS Extension Service, University of Florida undated.

4 Ballinger, Ray. *A History of Sugar Marketing Through 1974.* U.S. Department of Agriculture: Agricultural Economic Report No. 381. Washington, D.C. 1974.

5 "Smyrnea: Dr. Andrew Trumbull and the Mediterranean Settlement at New Smyrna and Edgewater, Florida, 1766-1777." *Florida History Online.* (See unf.edu)

6 https://edis.ifas.ufl.edu/pdffiles/AE/AE37500.pdf

7 Ballinger. *Ibid.,* p. 8.

8 https://en.wikibooks.org/wiki/History of Florida from Civil War to the Gilded Age, 1861-1900)

9 Ballinger, *Ibid.,* p. 76

10 United States Department of Agriculture, *Report of the Secretary of Agriculture, 1891.* Washington, D.C. 1892, p. 170.

11 Hitchman, James. "U.S. Control over Cuban Sugar Production 1898-1902." *Journal of Interamerican Studies and World Affairs.* Vol. 12, No. pp. 90-106 1970.

12 *Orlando Sentinel,* July 3, 2005.

13 See Hollander, Gail M., *Raising Cane in the Glades: The Global Sugar Trade and the Transformation of Florida.* University of Chicago Press: Chicago and London, 2008.

14 Ocala Evening Star, December 28, 1908.

15 Wright, J. O., *The Everglades of Florida: Their Adaptability for the Growth of Sugar Cane.* Tallahassee, 1912.

16 *Ibid* p. 83

17 *Ibid.*

[18] *Report of the Florida Everglades Engineering Commission to the Board of Trustee of the Everglades Drainage District and the Trustees of the Internal Improvement Fund State of Florida.* U.S. Government Printing Office, Washington, 194. p. 5.

[19] Grogan, Kevin. *Cuba's Dance of the Millions: Examining the Causes and Consequences of Violent Price Fluctuations in the Sugar Market Between 1919 and 1920.* Master's Thesis, University of Florida, 2004, p. 10.

[20] *Ibid.,* p. 27.

[21] These are full year totals. Price fluctuations varied widely from month to month during the Dance.

[22] Bethell, Leslie. *Cuba: A Short History.* Cambridge University Press, Cambridge, 1993. p. 47.

[23] Cuban Studies Institute, *This Day in History: November 1920—Collapse of the Dance of the Millions.* West Palm Beach, undated.

[24] *Palm Beach Weekly News,* March 22, 1912.

[25] Southern Sugar Company, brochure, 1929.

[26] Patterson, Gordon. "Raising Cane and Refining Sugar: Florida Crystals and the Fame of Fellsmere." *Florida Historical Quarterly,* Volume LXXV, Number 4, Spring, 1997. p. 411.

[27] *Ibid.,* p. 423.

[28] Hollander, *Ibid,* p. 86.

[29] *Ibid.* p. 86.

[30] https://www.marketplace.org/2017/08/24/what-was-one-worst-pieces-us-legislation/

[31] Ballinger, *Ibid.,* p. 32.

[32] U.S. Tariff Commission. *Sugar.* U.S. Government Printing Office, Washington, D.C., 1934.

[33] Ballinger, *Ibid.* p. 33.

[34] Wiltgen, Tyler James. *An Economic History of the United States Sugar Program.* M.S. thesis Montana State University, August 2007.p. 19.

[35] Ballinger, *Ibid.,*p. 34.

[36] Ballinger, *Ibid.,* p. 36.

[37] Heitmann, *Ibid.,* p. 54.

[38] USDA, Commodity Stabilization Service, Sugar Division, "Sugar Statistics and Data Compiled in the Administration of the Sugar Acts," *Statistical Bulletin 214,* July 1957.

[39] Hollander, *Ibid.,* p. 124. I use the term "neo-plantationism" directly from Hollander's book because it seems to describe, in one word, the trajectory of USSC's treatment of its resident workers.

[40] Ballinger, *Ibid.,* p. 40.

[41] Hearing before the Committee on Finance, United States Senate. *Amending Sugar Act of 1934.* United States Government Printing Office, Washington, D.C. March 18, 1941.

[42] *Ibid.* p. 11

[43] *Ibid.*

[44] *Ibid.,* p. 2.

[45] Pepper, Claude, *New York Times,* December 16, 1941.

[46] *Ibid.,* p. 41.

[47] *Ibid.,* p. 49.

[48] Hollander, *Ibid.,* p. 156.

[49] https://www.sugar.org/

[50] Briggs, Vernon. *Guestworker Programs: Lessons from the Past and Warnings for the Future.* Center for Immigration Studies, 2004, p.3.

[51] Carney, Timothy. "Not So Sweet." *The American Conservative,* June 5, 2006.

[52] See Hollander, *Ibid.,* p.137. This is her citation of Levine, L. Florida—Report of a visit on January 14 through January 26, 1942 to United States Employment Service Office.

[53] Khalil Gibran Muhammad and Tya Miles: "The 1619 Project." *New York Times.* https://www.nytimes.com/interactive/2019/08/14/magazine/sugar-slave-trade-slavery.html

[54] Ballinger, *Ibid.,* p. 53.

[55] See Hollander, *Ibid.,* p. 162

[56] The law at the time stated that only countries with diplomatic relationships could be considered for sugar quotas.

[57] As a personal note, the author was in the United States Army at the time and can attest to the fact that we were a hair breadth away from a nuclear holocaust.

[58] For an excellent expanded discussion of this point, see Hollander, *Ibid.* pp. 168-172.

[59] Cooley, Harold in a letter to Agriculture Secretary Orville Freeman, September 7, 1961.

[60] Montoya, Joseph in a letter to James Ralph, Assistant Secretary of Agriculture, November 15, 1961.

[61] United States Senate: *Hearings before the Committee on Finance.* May 29, 1962, p. 22.

[62] https://jamiemontilla.com/guanica

[63] https://jamiemontilla.com/usa-florida.

[64] *New York Times,* December 16, 1963.

[65] Hollander, *Ibid.,* p. 190

[66] From Hollander, *Ibid.,* p.187

[67] Florida Department of Agriculture and Consumer Services: *Viva Florida 500: History of Sugarcane.* February 15, 2013.

[68] Hollander, *Ibid,* p. 196.

[69] Ballinger, *Ibid.,* p. 77.

[70] http://chartsbin.com/view/44263

[71] Ballinger, *Ibid.,* p. 77.

[72] Keams, Cristin, Stanton A. Glantz, Laura A. Schmidt: *Sugar Industry Influence on the Scientific Agenda of the National Institute of Dental Research's 1971 National Caries Program: A Historical Analysis of Internal Documents.* March 10, 2015. https://doi.org/10.1371/journal.pmed.1001798

[73] Economic Research Service, United States Department of Agriculture: *Sugar and Sweetener Yearbook Tables.* https://www.ers.usda.gov/data-products/sugar-and-sweeteners-yearbook-tables/sugar-and-sweeteners-yearbook-tables/

[74] Flaherty, Peter, Deputy Attorney General. *Memorandum Opinion for the Secretary of Agriculture: Price Support for Sugar Producers—Agriculture Act of 1949.* August 18, 1977.

[75] *Ibid.,* pp.191-192.

[76] *Ibid.,* p. 193.

[77] https://www.govtrack.us/congress/bills/95/s275

[78] Governor Bob Graham in a letter to Senator Richard Stone. Florida State Archives.

[79] Public law 95-113—September 29, 1977, Title IX.

[80] *Ibid.*

[81] Economic Research Service, *Ibid.*

[82] *Ibid.*

[83] U.S. Congress: House Committee on Agriculture. *General Farm Bill of 1981*. 97th Congress, March 11, 1981, p. 39.

[84] Wiltgen. *Ibid.* p. 30.

[85] Barry, Robert, et al. *Sugar: Background for 1990 Farm Legislation*, p. 44. See www.ers. usda.gov/publications/pub-details/?pubid=41841

[86] https://www.govtrack.us/congress/bills/97/s884.

[87] Economic Research Service, *Ibid.*

[88] Lord, Ron. *Background for 1995 Farm Legislation*. Economic Research Service, USDA Report 711, p. 26.

[89] *Ibid.*, p. 4

[90] *Ibid.* p. 8.

[91] https://www.ussugar.com/railroad/

[92] Lord, *Ibid.*, p. 10.

[93] The Belle Glade processing plant had closed down in 1985.

[94] https://en.wikipedia.org/wiki/High-fructose_corn_syrup

[95] Barry, et al, *Ibid.*, p. 26.

[96] Buyken, Annette, Janina Goletzke, Gesa Joslowski, Anna Felbick, Guo Cheng, Christian Herder, Jennie C. Brand-Miller. "Association between carbohydrate quality and inflammatory markers: systematic review of observational and interventional studies." *The American Journal of Clinical Nutrition*, Volume 99, Issue 4, April 2014,

[97] Poppe, David. "Sweet Talk." *Florida Trend*, October 1, 1995

[98] https://www.ers.usda.gov/data-products/commodity-costs-and-returns

[99] Roka, F., Leslie Baucum and Jose Alvarez: *Costs and Returns for Sugarcane Production on Muck Soils in Southern Florida 2008 – 2009*. Gainesville: University of Florida Institute of Food and Agricultural Sciences, p. 4.

[100] Roka, F., Jose Alvarez and Leslie Baucum: *Costs and Returns for Sugarcane Production on Mineral Soils of South Florida, 2007 – 2008*. Gainesville: University of Florida Institute of Food and Agricultural Sciences.

[101] Roka, F., Leslie Baucum and Jose Alvarez: *Ibid.*

[102] The quality factor, or QF, converts net tons to net standard tons by adjusting for sucrose levels that may vary from the normative 12.5 per cent.

[103] These estimates are based upon national averages from USDA data. However, regional differences can occur and none of the data presented here can be traced to Florida.

[104] Much of the following discussion comes from ideas set forth in the University of Florida's IFAS *Costs and Returns for Sugarcane Production on Mineral Soils of South Florida, 2007 – 2008.*

[105] Lord, *Ibid.,* p. 29.

[106] *Ibid.,* p. 17.

[107] https://www.gao.gov/assets/160/153354.pdf

[108] *Ibid.,* p. 32.

[109] Hollander, *Ibid.,* p. 258

[110] Smith, Fran: *Sugar—Congress' Favorite Sweetener,* Competitive Enterprise Institute, December 9, 2013.

[111] Quanhe Yang, PhD et al: "Added Sugar Intake and Cardiovascular Diseases Mortality among US Adults," *Journal of the American Medical Association (JAMA),* April 2014.

[112] Briscoe, Andrew III and P. Courtney Gaine, PhD: *American Sugar Association 2015 Dietary Guidelines Advisory Committee,* December 12, 2014.

[113] Moss, Michael, *Salt, Sugar, Fat.* Random House, New York, 2013, p. 130.

[114] Ludwig, D., Peyterson, K., and Gortmaker, S.: "Relation between consumption of sugar-sweetened drinks and childhood obesity: a perspective, observational analysis." *The Lancet,* 2001.

[115] American Chemical Society. "Soda Warning? High-fructose Corn Syrup Linked To Diabetes, New Study Suggests." *Science Daily.* www.sciencedaily.com/releases/2007/08/070823094819.htm (accessed November 8, 2020).

[116] Email to the author from Dr. Steven Mason, cardiologist.

[117] Eboch, M. M.: *Inside the Sugar Industry.* Abdo Publishing, Minneapolis, 2017. pp. 50-51.

[118] Howard, Barbara and Judith Wylie-Rosett: *A Statement for Healthcare Professionals From the Committee on Nutrition of the Council on Nutrition, Physical Activity, and Metabolism of the American Heart Association.* July 2002.

[119] In *Circulation,* a publication of the American Heart Association. July 2009.

[120] Basu S, Yoffe P, Hills N, Lustig RH: "The Relationship of Sugar to Population-Level Diabetes Prevalence: An Econometric Analysis of Repeated Cross-Sectional Data." *PLoS ONE* 8(2): 2013

[121] George A Bray, Samara Joy Nielsen, Barry M Popkin, "Consumption of high-fructose corn syrup in beverages may play a role in the epidemic of obesity," *The American Journal of Clinical Nutrition,* Volume 79, Issue 4, April 2004, Pages 537–543, https://doi.org/10.1093/ajcn/79.4.537

122 Bray GA. Soft drink consumption and obesity: it is all about fructose. Curr Opin Lipidol. 2010 Feb;21(1):51-7. doi: 10.1097/MOL.0b013e3283346ca2. PMID: 19956074.

123 https://www.health.harvard.edu/heart-health/the-sweet-danger-of-sugar

124 *New York Times,* September 12, 2016

125 *New York Times,* August 9, 2015

126 Choi, Candice. *AP Exclusive: How candy makers shape nutrition science.* June 2, 2016.

127 White, John S. "Straight talk about high-fructose corn syrup: what it is and what it ain't," *The American Journal of Clinical Nutrition,* Volume 88, Issue 6, December 2008, Pages 1716S–1721S, https://doi.org/10.3945/ajcn.2008.25825B

128 https://www.linkedin.com/in/john-s-white-2a224219

129 Christine S. Tsilas, Russell J. de Souza, Sonia Blanco Mejia, Arash Mirrahimi, Adrian I. Cozma, Viranda H. Jayalath, Vanessa Ha, Reem Tawfik, Marco Di Buono, Alexandra L. Jenkins, Lawrence A. Leiter, Thomas M.S. Wolever Joseph Beyene, Tauseef Khan, Cyril W.C. Kendall, David J. A. Jenkins, and John L. Sievenpiper. "Relation of total sugars, fructose and sucrose with incident type 2 diabetes: a systematic review and meta-analysis of prospective cohort studies." *Canadian Medical Association Journal,* May 23, 2017.

130 Zieman, Joseph, James Fourqurean and Thoms Frankovich. "Seagrass Die-off in Florida Bay: Long-term Trends in Abundance and Growth of Turtle Grass." *Estuaries,* Vol. 22, No. 28, June 1999. p. 480.

131 Interview with Mary Barley, November 7, 2020.

132 Hirth, Diane. "Sugar TaxProposed to Save Glades." *Fort Lauderdale Sun-Sentinel.* September 30, 1993.

133 Kennedy, John. "Court Blocks Everglades-Cleanup Amendment from Ballot." *Orlando Sun-Sentinel.* May 27, 1994.

134 *Ibid.*

135 https://floridadep.gov/eco-pro/eco-pro/content/everglades-forever-act-efa

136 Florida Constitution, Art X, Sec-17

137 Klass, Mary Ellen. "Sugar's decades-long hold over Everglades came with a price." *Miami Herald,* July 11, 2016, updated July 12, 2016.

138 https://myfloridalegal.com/ago.nsf/ Opinions/9083F168C353A721852563F600673D09

139 An advisory opinion from a court is not binding but an expression of the court's sentiment on a matter; it is generally followed.

[140] https://www.usda.gov/data-products/sugar-and-sweeteners-yearbook-tables/#World%20and%20U.S.%20Sugar%20and%20Corn%20Sweetener%20Prices

[141] Klaas, Mary Ellen. *Tampa Bay Times.* July 15, 2016.

[142] Shapouri, Dr. Hosseini, OEPNU/OCE, USDA and Dr. Michael Salassi, J. Nelson Fairbanks Professor of Agricultural Economics, Department of Agricultural Economics and Agribusiness, LSU Agricultural Center. *The Economic Feasibility of Ethanol Production from Sugar in the United States.* July, 2006.

[143] https://www.sun-sentinel.com/news/fl-xpm-1985-07-10-8501280167-story.html

[144] https://www.courtlistener.com/opinion/1919977/okeelanta-corp-v-bygrave/

[145] Much of this information comes from multiple sources, but the primary source is a 2001 article in Vanity Fair magazine. For the full story please see https://www.vanityfair.com/news/2001/02/floridas-fanjuls-200102

[146] Barton, Eric. "Bitter Sugar." *Broward Palm Beach New Times.* August 26, 2004

[147] U.S. House *Report on the Use of Temporary Foreign Workers in the Florida Sugar Cane Industry.* Committee on Education and Labor. July 1991.

[148] McCabe, Robert. "Taking their Lumps." *South Florida Sun-Sentinel.* July 8,1991.

[149] General Accounting Office. *Foreign Farm Workers in the U.S.: Department of Labor Action Needed to Protect Florida Sugar Cane Workers.* June 1992.

[150] Bovard, James. *Cato Institute Policy Analysis No. 135: Farm Bill Follies of 1990.* Cato Institute, July 12, 1990.

[151] *Ibid.*

[152] Moore, Stephen and Dean Stansel. *Cato Institute Policy Analysis No. 225: Ending Corporate Welfare as We Know It.* Cato Institute, May 12, 1995.

[153] Letter from General Accounting Office dated June 9, 2000. Reference B-285072.

[154] https://www.aei.org/carpe-diem/protectionist-sugar-policy-cost-americans-3-billion-in-2012/

[155] Cole, Robert J. "Sugar Sale By G.&W." *New York Times*, October 6, 1984.

[156] Economic Research Service, *Ibid.*

[157] Jurenas, Remy. *Sugar Proposals for the 2012 Farm Bill.* Congressional Research Service, June 12, 2012.

[158] Economic Research Service, *Ibid.*

[159] For more information on this appointment please see the following https://www.tampabay.com/news/politics/gubernatorial/after-scotts-secret-trip-to-king-ranch-he-tapped-ranch-employee-for-state/2190920/

160 Smith, Fran. *Sugar—Congress' Favorite Sweetener.* Competitive Enterprise Institute, December 9, 2013.

161 Beghin, John and Amani Elobeid. *The Impact of the U.S. Sugar Program Redux.* Center for Agricultural and Rural Development Iowa State University Ames, Iowa May, 2013.

162 Beghin, John and Amani Elobeid. *Analysis of the U.S. Sugar Program.* American Enterprise Institute, November 6, 2107.

163 Dewey, Caitlin. "Why Americans Pay More for Sugar." *Washington Post,* June 8, 2017.

164 *Ibid.*

165 Dewey, Caitlin. *Washington Post.* June 9, 2017.

166 Naja, Melodie, Stephen Davis and Thomas Van Lent, *The Everglades Scientists Weigh in on Harmful Algae Blooms.* Everglades Foundation, 2018.

167 https://pubmed.ncbi.nlm.nih.gov/25904601/

168 "The Sugar Scandal: Congress takes a run at an egregious business welfare scheme." *Wall Street Journal,* July 29, 2015

169 This data comes from https://www.opensecrets.org, a part of the Center for Responsive Politics, and while it is as reliable a source as exists, it is never perfect and should be considered carefully.

170 *Ibid.*

171 https://floridalobbyist.gov/CompensationReportSearch/CompAggregateTotals/Full%20year%202019

172 https://www.cnn.com/ALLPOLITICS/time/1998/09/14/high.crimes.html

173 United States District Court, Southern District of Florida. Case No. 9:19-cv-80730-RS-MM

174 The current standard is 12 microns per cubic liter.

175 *State of Our Air: Our Commitment, Our Community.* U.S. Sugar Corporation, August 2019 – August 2020

176 *Sugar Industry Spreads Lies about its Toxic Sugarcane Burning Following Florida Residents' Lawsuit,* Oct 29, 2020. https://www.bermanlaw.com

177 https://www.epa.gov/pm-pollution/particulate-matter-pm-basics#effects

178 Case 9:19-cv-80730-RS Document 152 Entered on FLSD Docket 11/12/2020, p. 14.

179 H. S. Sandhu, R. A. Gilbert, G. Kingston, J. F. Subiros, K. Morgan, R. W. Rice, L. Baucum, J. M. Shine, Jr., and L. Davis. "Microclimate in Florida and Costa Rica." *Agr. Forest Meteorol.* 177: 101–109.

[180] Sandhu, Hardev S., Fermín, Subiros-Ruiz, Ronald W. Rice, James M. Shine, Jr. "Harvest management effects on sugarcane growth, yield and nutrient cycling in Florida and Costa Rica." *Field Crops Research,* December 2017, Pages 253-26.

[181] Nunez, Oscar and Egbert Spaans: "Evaluation of green-cane harvesting and crop management with a trash-blanket." *Sugar Tech* 10(1):29-35 March, 2008.

CPSIA information can be obtained
at www.ICGtesting.com
Printed in the USA
BVHW091923200521
607797BV00002B/183

9 781954 396012